Brooklyn.

Brooklyn. Once the overlooked middle child in New York's borough family, Brooklyn has shrugged off any inferiority complex to become the global capital of cool—where skateboards double as office desks or where a bodega cat might have more Instagram followers than you.

Brooklyn is a borough of contradictions. Luxury condos cast shadows over anarchist bookstores. Vegan bakeries coexist with 100-year-old pastrami-slinging delis. You'll find rooftop raves in Gowanus warehouses and backyard poetry readings in Bed-Stuy. Vintage is currency, and authenticity is curated with intent.

But beyond the kaleidoscope of clichés lies something magnetic. LOST iN introduces you to the locals who make the borough tick: the Coney Island native giving food tours from his vintage checkered cab, the Le Cordon Bleu–trained chef who left the line to cook in a Clinton Hill brownstone, the DJ weaving genre-spanning sets laced with sounds from the streets.

You'll discover where a new generation of car aficionados gather in a forgotten Navy Yard terminal, where to sip from a 13-glass martini fountain with escargot, and how to pick up skating at an intergalactic dream-rink lit like a spaceship landing. Brooklyn is messy and mythic. A borough forever under construction—of buildings, identities, dreams. Get lost in its maze of neighborhoods, its alchemy of edge and warmth. Get lost in Brooklyn.

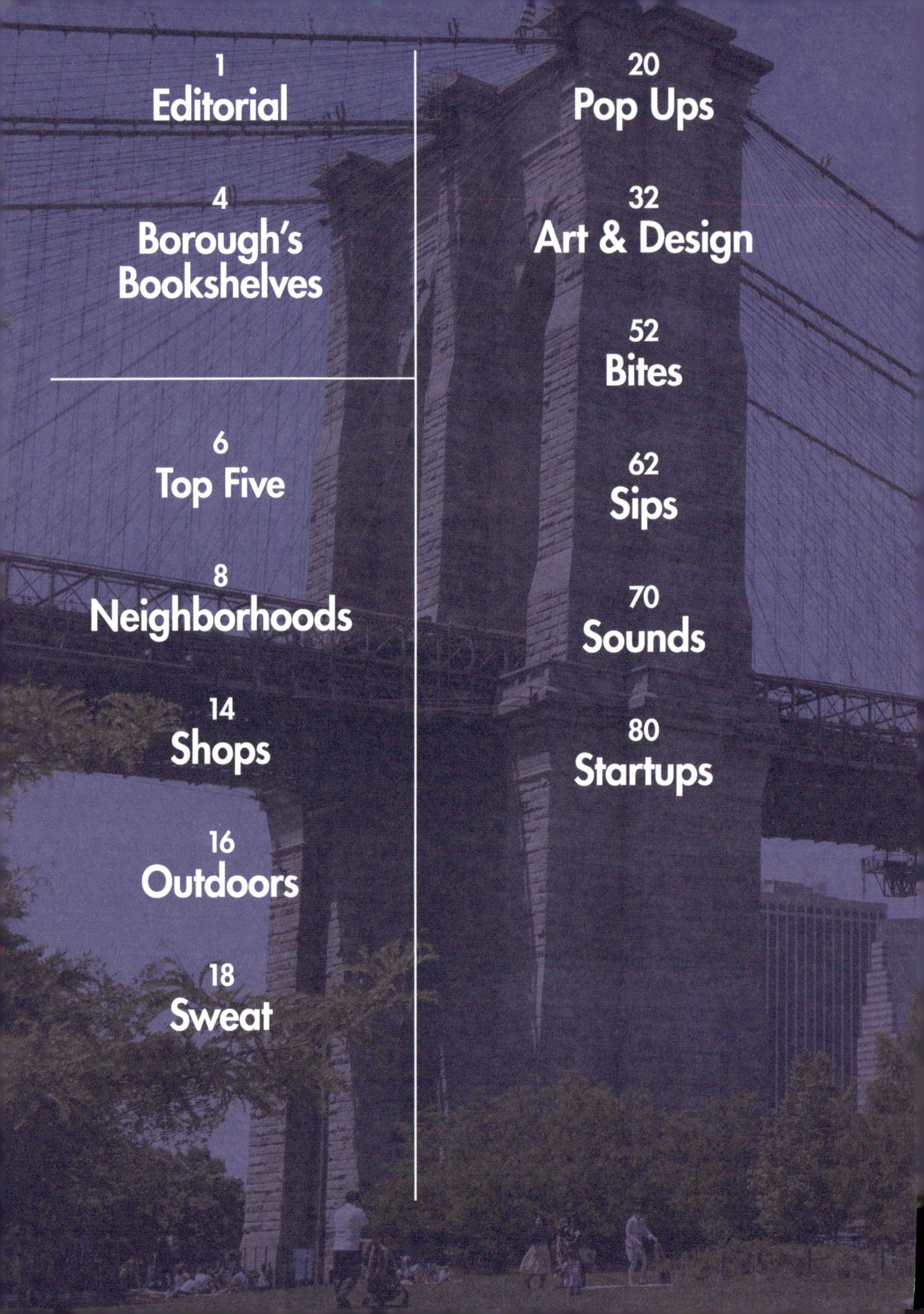

The Brooklyn Public Library's Central Library, located at Grand Army Plaza, is a striking example of Art Deco design. Its iconic limestone façade features gilded reliefs depicting great works of literature and knowledge. Inside, the building houses expansive reading rooms, archival collections and modern amenities like a business and career center, recording studio and public event spaces. Blending historic architecture with contemporary resources, it remains a vital hub for learning and community in Brooklyn. ∎

Central Library, 10 Grand Army Plaza, Prospect Heights

Grand Army Plaza is Brooklyn's grand gateway—an iconic arch, fountains and wide open space where historic charm meets city energy, linking Prospect Park to the borough's cultural and civic heart

Top Five

Our picks, inspired by Brooklyn's one-of-a-kind culture and style. Get lost in checking each of them off of your list.

Best Bagels
- ☐ Court Street Bagels
- ☐ Greenberg's Bagels
- ☐ Frankel's Delicatessen
- ☐ Knickerbocker Bagel
- ☐ Shelsky's Brooklyn Bagels

Best Bakery
- ☐ Bakeri
- ☐ Bien Cuit
- ☐ Burrow
- ☐ L'Appartement 4F
- ☐ Welcome Home

Best Cocktail Bar
- ☐ Bitter Monk
- ☐ Elsa
- ☐ The Clover Club
- ☐ Nicky's Unisex
- ☐ Maison Premiere

Best Outdoor Hang
- ☐ The backyard at With Others
- ☐ Domino Park
- ☐ Fort Greene Park
- ☐ Frog Wine Bar
- ☐ Nowadays

Best Bodega Snack
- ☐ Bacon, egg and cheese
- ☐ A chopped cheese from Hajji's
- ☐ The Nutcracker
- ☐ Sour straws from the candy rack
- ☐ Turkey club sandwich from Anthony & Son Panini Shoppe

Best Slice
- ☐ Best Pizza
- ☐ FINI Pizza
- ☐ L'Industrie Pizza
- ☐ Paulie Gee's
- ☐ Scarr's Pizza

Best Jazz Bar
- ☐ Cafe Erzulie
- ☐ Lowlands Bar
- ☐ LunÀtico
- ☐ Ornithology Jazz Club
- ☐ ShapeShifter Lab

Best Vintage Shopping
- ☐ 10 ft Single by Stella Dallas
- ☐ Awoke Vintage
- ☐ Beacon's Closet
- ☐ ÉMEUTE
- ☐ Stella Dallas Living

Best Rooftop Dinner
- ☐ Laser Wolf
- ☐ Westlight
- ☐ Kimoto Rooftop
- ☐ LilliStar at Moxy
- ☐ Cherry on Top

Best Date Spot
- ☐ Hotel Delmano
- ☐ Rhodora Wine Bar
- ☐ Maison Premiere
- ☐ Bar Bête
- ☐ Zig Zag

Around Town

Brooklyn's Little Poland

Greenpoint, one of Brooklyn's most sought-after neighborhoods to live and play, is a fascinating blend of old and new, where industrial roots meet modern creativity. In the 1900s, this northernmost neighborhood in Brooklyn was a thriving hub for manufacturing and shipbuilding. A wave of Polish immigrants followed, earning the area the nickname "Little Poland." That legacy still runs strong: feast on pierogi from *Pierozek*, and don't miss the *paczek* (Polish donuts) from *Syrena Bakery*. Today, Greenpoint is equally defined by its cool, creative edge. You'll find historic churches and rustic taverns side by side with natural wine bars, Michelin-starred restaurants and trendy boutiques. Design studios occupy converted warehouses and new high-rises increasingly line the waterfront. Spend the day vintage shopping near McCarren Park, grabbing donuts from *Peter Pan Donut & Pastry Shop*, and catching the sunset at *WNYC Transmitter Park*. The options for dinner are limitless, but *Greenpoint Fish & Lobster Co.* is always a solid bet. After dark, dance to disco at *Ponyboy* or head to the *Good Room* for more driving beats. ■

Greenpoint

Credit: MusikAnimal, CC BY-SA 4.0, via Wikimedia Commons

The Melting Pot

Did you know that New York City has a lesser-known Fifth Avenue, one that pulses with Latin American culture? In Sunset Park, juicy al pastor is piled atop handmade tortillas at *Tacos El Bronco*, a beloved truck serving authentic Mexican eats. A few blocks down, *Sabor de Colombia* serves *pan de bono*—that delectable, chewy, slightly sweet cheese bread. Meanwhile, Eighth Avenue is home to one of the fastest-growing ethnic Chinese enclaves outside of Asia. Along the street, you'll find outdoor fruit stands next to tanks of live fish, dried medicinal herbs next to bubble tea shops, and whole barbecued duck hanging in display cases next to dumpling joints like *Kai Feng Fu*. At the top of the hill, the neighborhood's eponymous park offers sweeping views of the sunset and Manhattan skyline. It's not uncommon to see vendors pushing carts of paletas as elderly locals practice tai chi nearby. Despite language barriers, a shared sense of community unites Sunset Park's diverse residents as they come together to watch another day fade away. ■

Sunset Park

Island Time

Since the 1960s, immigrants from Jamaica, Haiti, Trinidad and beyond have brought their music, language and flavors to Flatbush, resulting in the largest and most diverse Caribbean American community outside of the West Indies. An ideal day in Brooklyn's Little Caribbean starts with warm currant rolls from *Allan's Bakery* and housemade sorrel juice from *Lips Cafe*. Across the street you'll find *Aunts et Uncles*, an impeccably designed lifestyle shop and plant-based cafe that is deeply rooted in the community. At *Flatbush Central Caribbean Marketplace*, local vendors sell everything from records to natural skin products to colorful Panamanian apparel. Be sure to pay a visit to *BunNan*, where chef/owner Nadège Fleurimond is championing Haitian cuisine through all things plantain. As you take in the sounds of soca and reggae weaving with the scent of jerk chicken from *Peppa's*, keep an eye out for vibrant street art. Finally, catch a performance at *Kings Theatre*, a breathtakingly restored concert hall inspired by Parisian architecture. ■

Flatbush

Wasteland to Wonderland

Stretching just shy of two miles, the Gowanus Canal was once one of the most polluted waterways in the country. But thanks to a major environmental cleanup initiative that began in 2013, the area has transformed into one of Brooklyn's hotspots to eat, drink, shop and play. Kickstart your day with a seasonal beverage at *Beanmonger Coffee*, followed by freshly baked treats at *Sixteen Mill Bakeshop*. From there, embark on a brewery crawl to local favorites like *Finback Brewery* and *Wild East Brewing Company*. Later, dive into the Gowanus creative scene with a live show at *The Bell House*. Or if you prefer your creativity on a plate and in a coupe, check out *Claro* for elevated Oaxacan plates and *Dirty Precious* for craft cocktails. *Royal Palms Shuffleboard Club* is a classic destination for late-night fun. If you're in the mood to groove, make your way to *Public Records*, a top-tier sound venue. Between the lush Atrium and immersive Sound Room, audiophiles and bassheads alike will rejoice. ■

Gowanus

Tucked away in southwest Brooklyn, Red Hook isn't easy to reach, but that contributes to its charm. Its relative isolation has allowed artists and makers, brewers and distillers, restaurateurs and bakers to transform the once-crumbling waterfront into a vibrant, self-sustaining community. Many of the area's old shipping warehouses have found new life as creative spaces, like the *Brooklyn Waterfront Artists Coalition* and *Pioneer Works*, a multidisciplinary art and science center. Others serve as homes to iconic local booze brands. Sip regional ales at *Strong Rope Brewery*, sample small-batch bourbon at *Widow Jane Distillery*, or swirl a vintage from the North Fork of Long Island at *Red Hook Winery*—you'll never go thirsty here. You won't go hungry, either: *Brooklyn Crab* and *Red Hook Lobster Pound* serve casual, high-quality seafood, while *Red Hook Tavern* (pictured) is home to one of the city's best burgers. Grab dessert at *Steve's Authentic Key Lime Pie* and watch the sun dip behind Lady Liberty from Valentino Pier. Finally, meander along the cobblestone streets to *Sunny's Bar*, a beloved century-old institution with live music almost every night. ■

Red Hook

Eastern European Enclave

Two months before filming began for the Oscar-winning *Anora*, director Mike Baker moved his entire team to Brighton Beach. The result is a love letter to this Eastern European enclave in South Brooklyn and the immigrant communities that have settled there. Long before *Williams Candy*, a neighborhood fixture since the 1940s, lit up the silver screen in *Anora*, it was a local favorite for Brooklyn Cyclones fans during home games. Further down the boardwalk, art imitates life at *Tatiana*, where vodka flows endlessly and dinner is accompanied by a Vegas-style show. The *Riegelmann Boardwalk* was not portrayed in all its glory. This three-mile stretch comes alive in the summer, beginning with the annual Mermaid Parade in June and continuing through August with fireworks every Friday night. For the ultimate fireworks experience, grab a hot dog from *Nathan's Famous* and a pint of Mermaid Pilsner, and catch the show from atop the Wonder Wheel. Cap off your visit with a trip to *Tashkent Supermarket*, tucked beneath the elevated subway tracks at Brighton Beach Station. The hot food bar features Uzbek *plov* and *manti* next to Ukrainian cabbage rolls and Russian potato salad—a cornucopia of cuisines that reflects the diversity of the people who call Brighton Beach home. ∎

Brighton Beach

Once the site of several Revolutionary War forts, Fort Greene is now a vibrant cultural cornerstone of Brooklyn. Stroll down tranquil streets where majestic trees tower over landmarked brownstones, many of which carry a rich legacy of Black artistry. Among the neighborhood's most famous residents was Zora Neale Hurston, one of the 20th century's most celebrated African American writers. Later came Spike Lee, who brought the neighborhood's stories to the screen, and the bohemian wave of the 1980s and 1990s. The neighborhood has changed since then, but its artistic pulse remains strong. Catch cutting-edge theater at the *Brooklyn Academy of Music* or a cult classic at the *Alamo Drafthouse*. On Saturdays, the *Fort Greene Park Greenmarket* bustles with local makers and fresh produce. Along Myrtle Avenue, long-standing staples like *Castro's*, *LaRina Pastificio & Vino* and *Putnam's Pub* are as much third places as they are excellent eateries. Meanwhile, newcomers like *Third Falcon* and *Strange Delight* are shaping Fort Greene's ever-evolving culinary scene. ■

Fort Greene

A Gritty Past

Perhaps no neighborhood better symbolizes the reinvention—and the gentrification—of Brooklyn than Williamsburg. Throughout the 20th century, the former industrial hub attracted many waves of immigrants, including a large number of Puerto Ricans and a significant Hasidic Jewish population. Experience both cultures in South Williamsburg with a heaping plate of pastrami at kosher deli *Gottlieb's*, followed by drinks and dancing at *Tonita's*, the Caribbean social club, a cultural holdout from when the area was nicknamed "Los Sures." Recent decades saw artists flock to the neighborhood, drawn by cheap lofts and the glittering East River skyline, sparking an ongoing development boom. These days, Michelin-starred restaurants, buzzy cocktail bars and stylish boutiques might have you convinced you're in Soho. However, traces of Williamsburg's grittier past remain if you know where to look. There's *The Broadway*, an intimate bar often hosting underground music sets, and *Union Pool*, a dive bar continuing its legacy of punk, indie and experimental shows. Don't miss Reverend Vince Anderson & The Love Choir preaching their "dirty gospel," an experience more spiritual than religious, every Monday night for free. ■

Williamsburg

Cozy Reading Nooks

Brooklyn's indie bookshops are more than retail stores—they're cultural hubs that reflect the vibrancy of their communities. From *WORD* in Greenpoint to *Books Are Magic* in Cobble Hill and *Greenlight Bookstore* in Fort Greene, these are places to linger, read and gather. Sip on a coffee over intersectional feminist literature at *Cafe con Libros* or take an incense-making workshop at Bed-Stuy's *Adanne Bookshop,* where authors of color are spotlighted. At *Liz's Book Bar* in Carroll Gardens, books come with a glass of wine. And in Downtown Brooklyn, the *Center for Fiction* (pictured) anchors the local literary community with its bookstore, library, café/bar and writer's studio. ■

Various, see Index, p. 94

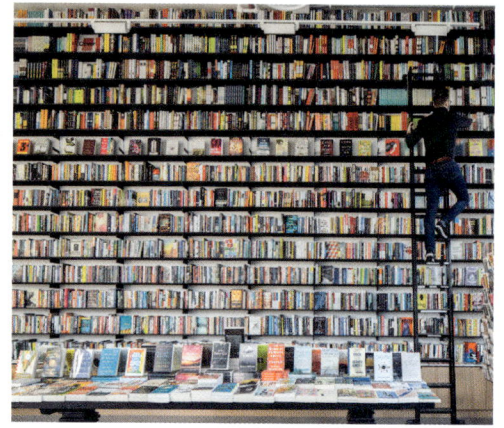

Shops

'Til You Drop

Mom-and-pop shops are the lifeblood of Brooklyn. Built by locals for locals, these spots embody the spirits of their neighborhoods, often doubling as third spaces where communities come to shop, gather and play

Other People's Closets

Brooklyn is one of the best places in the city to shop other people's closets. Stepping into *Unearth Vintage* (pictured) feels like entering a cozy living room: colorful mannequins in the window, mid-century furniture throughout, and walls lined with leather jackets and denim gems. Meanwhile, *Brooklyn Vintques* emulates an eclectic garage sale offering everything from vintage jerseys to jewelry to vinyl. For those who treat thrifting like a sport, *L Train Vintage* delivers the thrill of the hunt. Get lost among the racks of affordable streetwear and retro finds, and emerge with a new outfit that's uniquely you. ■

Various, see Index, p. 94

Cool Concepts

Some of the borough's most hidden gems are its concept stores—highly curated boutiques that cater to niche audiences. Take *Tenant* (pictured), for example. Located between Bed-Stuy and Bushwick, this sleek shop is devoted entirely to NYC's skateboarding scene. A few blocks away, the minimalist *Sincerely, Tommy* offers eclectic womenswear, one-of-a-kind home goods and other homages to global craftsmanship. Turn the concept into a lifestyle at *Che*, its sister eatery in Bed-Stuy, where seasonal vegetables and natural wine get the spotlight. ■

Various, see Index, p. 94

Sip and Savor

Brooklyn is a mecca for natural and organic wine lovers. Take *Stranger Wines* (pictured), founded by Andrew Tarlow, a pioneer of the borough's artisanal food scene. This Williamsburg bottle shop houses a thoughtful selection of wines from small, sustainable producers around the world. Over in Bed-Stuy, community is the focus at *Happy Cork*, which boasts the country's largest assortment of Black and minority-owned wine and spirits. And for booze-free fun, head to *Minus Moonshine* in Prospect Heights or Greenpoint, where shelves are stocked with non-alcoholic wines and functional beverages that lift your spirits—no buzz required. ■

Various, see Index, p. 94

Around the Corner

In New York City, bodegas are hallowed ground. More than just corner stores, they're go-tos for everything from pantry essentials to cleaning supplies to midnight cravings. You're not a local until you're on a first-name basis with the staff, and you're not truly a regular until the shop cat acknowledges you. Start your day with a bacon, egg and cheese; end your night with a halal platter over rice. If you're in Red Hook at the Clinton Street bodega (pictured), grab a chopped cheese "the Ocky way"—you might even rub shoulders with Big Sean or Ed Sheeran while waiting for your ludicrously stuffed sandwich at this unmarked bodega.

• Various Locations

Rooftop Agriculture

Perched high above Brooklyn's industrial water-front, *Brooklyn Grange*'s rooftop farms are revolutionizing urban agriculture. With over five acres of rooftop soil farms—the largest in the world—this green roofing pioneer produces over 100,000 pounds of organic vegetables annually, with nearly 60% distributed to New Yorkers at low or no cost. Explore the farms on a public tour or take in breathtaking views of the Manhattan skyline while practicing sunset yoga, offered at the Navy Yards location during the summer months. ■

Brooklyn Grange, 63 Flushing Avenue & 850 Third Avenue, brooklyngrangefarm.com

Outdoors

Urban Oases

Outdoor spaces in Brooklyn vary widely: some expansive, others spanning a few steps; some grounded in nature, others soaring from the rooftops. All provide respite from the chaos of the concrete jungle—places to breathe, relax and grow

Public Living Room

Brownstones, named for their iconic chocolate-hued facades, have become a symbol of Brooklyn's architectural charm. But it's the stoops—those regal staircases leading to the front door—that truly define local culture. Originally designed to keep homes away from the muck of carriage horses, stoops have evolved into extensions of living rooms, blurring the lines between public and private. Whether you're drinking your morning coffee while people-watching on a tree-lined street in Park Slope or gathering with neighbors to sip wine in Bed-Stuy, stoop culture turns interior lives outward, inviting passersby to share in the joy of community. ■

Various Locations

Brooklyn's Backyard

To experience Brooklyn like a local, head to *Prospect Park*. Spanning over 500 acres with 30,000 trees, Brooklyn's answer to Central Park is the borough's backyard. Join the throngs of runners, walkers and cyclists on the 3.35-mile inner loop, or relax with a picnic and outdoor movie on the Great Lawn. Attend a live concert at the bandshell, or shop local at the *Grand Army Plaza Greenmarket* on Saturdays. From April to October, sample from dozens of local food vendors at *Smorgasburg*. Year-round, Prospect Park has something for everyone. ■

Prospect Park, prospectpark.org

Beneath the Freeway

Driving over the Kosciuszko Bridge on a Friday night, you might not be aware of the scene unfolding beneath the Brooklyn-Queens Expressway. This industrial stretch is one of the borough's newest public spaces by day and an exciting rave venue by night, when the freeway's steel beams glow with strobes and its concrete pillars reverberate with heavy bass. You're more likely to find out about sets from Resident Advisor than a venue website. Come prepared to dance the night away as the city rushes by overhead, none the wiser. ■

Under the K, Kosciuszko Bridge, East Williamsburg, nbkparks.org/under-the-k

For All Seasons

Perhaps best known for its 200+ cherry trees that bloom in spring, Brooklyn's largest garden is a treat for the senses all year round. In summer, savor the aroma of thousands of roses at the Cranford Rose Garden and the tranquility of the Japanese Hill-and-Pond Garden with its water lotus and koi. Fall brings the golden canopy of the ginkgo trees, while winter brings the festive twinkles of the holiday lights show. No matter the season, the sights and scents of the *Brooklyn Botanic Garden* await. ■

Brooklyn Botanic Garden, 150 Eastern Parkway, Prospect Heights, bbg.org

Moment of Zen

A visit to *Bathhouse* melts away stress for a modest day-pass rate (add-on treatments are available—we love the Moroccan-style hammam). Stop by for *aufguss*, a guided dry-sauna session. Wade in the ambient thermal pools, or gaze at a night sky replica in the Starlit Steam Room. There's a basalt stone–heated banya and selection of saunas, including one that mimics tropical temperatures. Just bring your bathing suit and water bottle: locker rooms are fully stocked with toiletries, towels and slippers. Open early morning to midnight. ■

Bathhouse, 103 North 10th Street, Williamsburg, abathhouse.com

Sweat

Good for You

When they're not trying to beat their last best step count, city dwellers may find themselves unwinding solo in a starlit steam room or lacing up bedazzled skates among friends. Meet the magical world of Brooklyn wellness and workouts, where the unconventional is status quo

The OG Run Club

Riverside 5Ks or jogs through saturated city blocks, running is a beloved and virtually free New York activity. With the surge of trendy run clubs, one has stayed true. Founded in 1970, *Prospect Park Track Club* was created with inclusivity as an intrinsic value. PPTC offers multiple weekly group runs around the park and up to two complimentary trial runs. Yearly membership costs $25. Then there's *Brooklyn Running Company*, a long-standing community shop that has free footwear fittings and lists 40+ local, themed running clubs on their site. ■

Various, see Index, p. 94

All the Asanas

With yoga studios on seemingly every other block, there are ample ways to expand your practice. *Yo BK* (pictured) is a hot yoga and pilates studio based in Greenpoint and Williamsburg, with outdoor events like silent discos on deck. *Kula Yoga Project*, a haven near the busy Radegast Hall, has been a mainstay for over a decade with their signature Honey Flow and self-love classes. Visit the newly independent *Fyra Yoga*, formerly Modo Yoga, a go-to for hot yogis in the borough. Book on ClassPass, Mindbody or directly. ■
Various, see Index, p. 94

Come Skate Away

If you know, you know. *Xanadu Roller Arts* is a self-described "intergalactic cruise ship" and source of multigenerational joy. Step inside and you're immediately transported to a retro-futuristic dreamscape that combines a rink, music venue and time warp all in one. Picture vibey 1970s-era wallpaper, pleasing printed fabrics and a hand-painted wood floor where you groove on eight wheels to the sounds of CHROMEO. From the creative mind of New York business owner Varun Kataria, the space operates on an events schedule, so check their calendar for the ideal vibe to power your roll. ■
Xanadu Roller Arts, 262 Starr Street, Bushwick, xanadu.nyc

Rock Stars

Scale a wall after the bars close at 4am, or bring the kids by for a wholesome afternoon. This space has everything. Day passes to *VITAL Climbing Gym* include unlimited indoor bouldering and one class from rooftop yoga to high-intensity cycling. There's a full gym on-site with slacklines, weights and specialized equipment to up your climbing skills. Shoe rentals, chalk bags and mats are available to rent 24/7. When you're not moonlighting as Tenzing Norgay, sign up for aerial silk classes with VITAL's in-house experts. ■
VITAL Climbing Gym, 221 N 14th Street, Williamsburg, vitalclimbinggym.com/brooklyn

Credit: Morrigan McCarthy

"Grab a ticket and a friend" for an evening with *that dinner thing*—bringing a friend, required. Mingle and meet locals while enjoying a themed dinner in a to-be-disclosed location

Credit: Claire Chalinover

Pop Ups

Brooklyn's neighborhoods pulse with community and flavor, from sizzling supper clubs to breezy flea markets and farm-fresh greenmarkets. Here, streets become dance floors, dinners feel like home, and every weekend offers a new taste of connection, creativity, and shared experience in the heart of the borough.

Local Flavor

Weekend memories are made where Brooklynites meet. Sip cider in Fort Greene and view classic cars at Wheels NYC. Make flea market discoveries and nosh on local bites. Come hungry, leave with a full heart

Credit: GrowNYC Greenmarket

Garden of Eatin'

Every Saturday, the *Fort Greene* (pictured) and *McCarren Park Greenmarkets* transform into hubs for fresh produce. Fort Greene, nestled among the park's chestnut trees, features local goods like hard cider from the *New York Cider Company*, farmstead kimchee from *Kimchee Harvest* and farm-raised trout from *Hudson Valley Fish Farm*. Vino squeezed from Long Island grapes adds a touch of local luxury. Meanwhile, McCarren Park serves up Sunday gravy ingredients from *City Saucery* alongside honey and soap from *Finger Lakes Beekeeping*. Year-round, the markets connect Brooklynites with New York State farmers. ■

Saturdays, various locations, see Index p. 94

Hot Wheels

Wheels of NYC is dedicated to classic and modified cars. While they host meetups across the five boroughs, their crown-jewel event—the Spring Classic—only happens at the Brooklyn Navy Yard. Recently, the group introduced fashion, music and design to flesh out the unique flavor of the city's car culture. Art cars and rare classic exotics are just the start. Recent partners in Wheels' ever-expanding footprint include *Alfargos Marketplace* for curated clothing and vintage watches, *Candylab* for a unique kids' zone, and fresh eats from *Leon's Bagels* and *Davey's Ice Cream*. ■

Wheels of NYC, various locations, wheelsof.com

Brooklyn Bazaars

Discover *Brooklyn Flea* in DUMBO—a breezy, bustling market under the Manhattan Bridge in the Dumbo Archway, packed with vintage gems, handcrafted treasures and mouthwatering bites. Soak up the lively market energy every Saturday and Sunday with a mix of curious locals and visitors. Then check out their newest creation, *BQ Flea*, beneath the BQE in Williamsburg/Greenpoint. Every Sunday, dive into a vibrant maze of 50+ vendors, scoring one-of-a-kind finds while reveling in the gritty-chic vibe of this freshly minted thrifting hotspot. Two markets, endless possibilities—come hunt, eat and wander. ■

Various, see Index p. 94

Dinner's Served

Indulge in *Heirloom Supper Club*'s (pictured) nostalgically crafted vegan dishes, each evoking cherished family dinners. Host your own soirée at *Frank's House*, a restored Greek Revival Brooklyn brownstone, boasting a kitchen equipped with the latest cooking accouterments. Or chase culinary adventure at *that dinner thing*, where wildly inventive monthly themes—like "duality" and "expansion"—inspire fiercely sought-after tickets (think sneaker-drops). But these gatherings offer more than hype: they're where strangers become lifelong friends or new partners. Two unique supper clubs and one retro venue, each delivering unforgettable flavors and deep human connection. ■

Various, see Index p. 94

Gina Bruno Knopov, Chef

Home Cooking

Gina Bruno Knopov
A graduate of Pratt Institute, Gina started her career in the art world, which eventually led her to the food scene. She and her husband now run *Frank's House*, a space for dinners, weddings and events in a charming Brooklyn brownstone

Starting in Brooklyn kitchens and refining her craft at Le Cordon Bleu in Paris, Gina carved her own path through grit, flavor and heart. Today, she brings that same spirit to *Frank's House*—a cozy, collaborative space where food and community meet. Here, she shares some of the unmissable eats in the borough

Tell us a little about your professional background as a chef.

My first job was in a sandwich shop. I got fired within the first two months because I showed up one day with a smile on my face, but clearly hung over. Then I stepped right into a small-scale Brooklyn place called *Leland*. I was split between the line and helping their baking program, which was awesome for a newbie because I was really getting two different types of experiences. While I was in that restaurant I was trying to run *Frank's House* at the same time, which was not called Frank's House. And ultimately, you can't answer emails and texts while on a line.

From there, I went to *Misi* in Brooklyn. Also on the line and very much on display, which I realized I loved very much. I loved being the showcase chef and everyone watching. I was there for a bit, just under a year. It was an absolutely wonderful experience. And it was a very tight-run kitchen. It was scary in the best way possible. Missy is an unbelievable chef and a fantastic person to learn from, but she's terrifying. I still salute her. While I was at Misi, my husband and I started to construct what is now Frank's House. I timed our little small launch of Frank's House to when I was going to leave Misi.

Do you feel that breaking into the cheffing business in Brooklyn is different than in other cities?

Being in Brooklyn is probably one of the better cities to decide you want to go into food because there is so much opportunity. Even the higher-end restaurants are looking for people, so you can easily get your foot in the door; even if you have to clean dishes, you're still in that kitchen and you're still absorbing things. The other side of it is that because it has such an impressive reputation, it is difficult. It is really, really difficult. It is extremely laborious. You are working with incredible ingredients, but it's higher stakes. God forbid you mess something up.

Ingredients are getting very expensive everywhere, especially here. What has the industry's response been?

I salute the restaurants that are buying quality ingredients and spending the price, but that just means the prices that you pay to sit there are going to be exorbitant. I've noticed some restaurants are putting where the beef was raised or where we bought the eggs on the menu—noting "this is a local farm" to reiterate, "Hey, we're spending these prices and it's really good quality." And that's why a burger is close to 40 bucks, which is nuts.

You studied at Le Cordon Bleu in Paris. What was that experience like?

It was completely in French and I do not speak French, but somehow you figure out what they're saying when they're showing you—it's such a visual act. That was an amazing experience, just being in Paris. Then I came back pregnant and now we have a one-year-old and I run Frank's House solo mission.

How would you describe Frank's House to a total stranger?

Frank's is meant to feel as if you're stepping into somebody's home. It is primarily an event space. The whole concept is that it is this home where you get to do your own pop-up. You know, everyone's apartment for the most part is on the smaller side, whether you're living in Manhattan or Brooklyn, and Frank's is that opportunity to do these dinners and feel as if you're doing them in your home. Frank is my father and he owns the building, hence the name.

Credit: Ally Rabon

Frank's House is the multi-faceted—pop-up dinner, micro wedding ceremony or branded event space in a restored Brooklyn brownstone

What's a favorite event you've hosted?

I just did a fantastic event with Creed, the fragrance company, and I teamed up with Molly Ford, who is a pretty well-known Brooklyn-based florist. I was the chef and they put together a floral bouquet workshop. It was a lovely group of 40 women. I feel like anytime you bring that many women together, it's just a really happy room.

Are there any new restaurants or businesses that you feel are really making a splash in the community?

Top of mind would be a place called *Theodora*; they also have a bakery called *Thea*. That is for sure number one. One owner is from Israel and the other is from Mexico City, and they nailed the perfect combination of flavors from each of those places into all their dishes. It is very difficult to get in, but it's an amazing experience.

I've been gravitating to *Place des Fêtes*, PDF, also in Clinton Hill. The owners also just opened *Café Mado*, which is also an excellent experience.

What are some classic favorites?

Four Horsemen. Forever a favorite. *Hart's*. Tiny, tiny little hole in the wall, but the food is phenomenal. *Vinegar Hill House*, also a classic. They have three different dining experiences. A backyard, a basement; it's very cool in there.

Taqueria Ramirez. Probably the best tacos I've ever had in Brooklyn. In New York, not just Brooklyn.

I'm checking out *The Snail* tonight, which is said to be very good.

Any favorite boutiques or second-hand stores or vintage shops?

Some favorite secondhand places for fashion are *Mirth Vintage*, *Raggedy Threads* and *Crossroads*. On

Crossroads Trading
Williamsburg

Seven Wonders Collective
Greenpoint

Dobbin St. Vintage Co-op
Greenpoint

Lichen NYC
Queens

Humble House
Greenpoint

L&B Spumoni Gardens
Bensonhurt

L'Industrie
Williamsburg

Best Pizza
Williamsburg

Ops
Bushwick

Chrissy's Pizza
Greenpoint

Lucali
Carroll Gardens

the home front, I like *Seven Wonders* and *Dobbin Street Vintage Co-op*, as well as *Lichen NYC* and *Humble House*.

What's your favorite mode of transportation in Brooklyn?
Citi Bike.

If someone's coming to visit Brooklyn, what's something they should understand about it?
My knee-jerk reaction is to tell them that it is so different from Manhattan. Like heavily. Brooklyn compared to Manhattan feels like a rural country. There are trees and backyards and green. There's so much green that you can't walk without sneezing during allergy season.

It has everything you need here. People are happier. It obviously is fast-paced, but it still has that neighborhood feel, and it's massive. There are so many things to explore in Brooklyn.

It's hard to talk about the borough without bringing up pizza.

What are some of your places of choice?
I am a pizza fanatic. I think Brooklyn pizza is pretty special. I would say if I had to have one slice of pizza and that was it for the rest of my life, I would be driving deep, deep into Sheepshead Bay, Brooklyn, and I would be getting *L&B Spumoni Gardens*.

If I want a slice, I'm definitely either a *L'Industrie* or a *Best* girl, both in Williamsburg. If I want a sit-down pizza, I love this place in Bushwick called *Ops*.

Shout out to *Chrissy's*; they recently opened and they're crushing pizzas. And *Lucali* still has my heart.

Any general travel advice to throw out?
Do all your traveling before you pop out a kid! But also, I eat through my travels. Maybe that's very on the nose for being in food. But I think when you travel, you taste culture. Depending on where you're going, you get a knowledge of everyone's different culture. ∎

I Hope Heaven Is a Brooklyn Summer

Matthew Allen

Brooklyn concerts chronicled through the years from Matthew's Nokia flip phone

When I found out about Brooklyn's weekly summer concerts, I was flabbergasted. At the time I moved there, I'd attended only one concert in my whole life—Alicia Keys at the New York State Fair in 2003. But when I realized that my favorite artists from the 1970s would be performing, I was stupefied. Free concerts? All summer?

I moved to Brooklyn on October 1, 2004.

Following a beautiful four years at Long Island University at C.W. Post Campus, I packed my suitcase full of clothes, CDs and Nintendo 64 video games to set down roots in Bedford-Stuyvesant. During college, I visited the borough a fair number of times. I marveled at its historic brownstones and delicious, crispy, cheese pizza slices.

In the first four months, I looked for work. Mind you, it was 2004, so there were no smartphones or tablets. I had to rely on a primitive resource called the classified section of the local newspaper. While my girlfriend was at work, I hopped on the subway, looking for my own job. I vividly remember getting lost transferring from the G train to the E train at Court Square in Queens one day, and on another day, I got so confused by the transit corn maze known as Atlantic Terminal that I just got out and walked around downtown Brooklyn. Back then, it was a train depot for the Long Island Railroad, but today, Barclays Center is there in its place.

As a 22-year-old born and raised in Syracuse, NY, I was drawn to Brooklyn, ironically, because of its differences and similarities to the 'Cuse. For instance, the housing projects in Brooklyn were big high-rises instead of the one-floor, two-bedroom projects from my hometown where some of my cousins lived. But the vibe outside was familiar: kids playing; men smoking and carrying on; kids' birthday parties with thin, colorful tablecloths and helium balloons blowing through the breeze as music blasted through car speakers.

I eventually found a job in Williamsburg as a customer service representative at CitiStorage, a box storage and courier company. It was a placeholder job to help pay bills while I continued to look for TV gigs, but CitiStorage was right on the waterfront of the East River. I walked from the L train Bedford Avenue stop to Brooklyn's best view of the Manhattan skyline five days a week.

Because I made just enough money to pay bills and get groceries, I had to find fun and unwind in frugal ways. My favorite thing in the world is music. At that time, I needed music to soundtrack every aspect of my life. Back then, I listened to music on my portable Sony Discman. Imagine being able to listen to only one album at a time. The humanity, I tell you! I was so attached to music that when my Discman broke, I used my portable DVD player to listen to my copy of Michael Jackson's *Off the Wall* on my way to job interviews.

When I found out about Brooklyn's weekly summer concerts, I was flabbergasted. At the time I moved there, I'd attended only one concert in my whole life—Alicia Keys at the New York State Fair in 2003. But when I realized that my favorite artists from the 1970s would be performing, I was stupefied. Free concerts? All summer?

On July 21, 2005, I attended my first free concert at Wingate Field, in the shadow of Crown Heights' Kings County Hospital. Wingate had a unique place in hip-hop history. The high school that the field belonged to was where legendary MCs Monie Love and MC Lyte had met nearly two decades before. On that day, I sat on the splintered wooden bleachers, unfazed by being all the way in the back and the bands looking like blurry ants with guitars and trumpets. For decades, Slave was first. My smile grew wide and tight as they played funk classics like "Watching You," "Just a Touch of Love" and "Weak in the Knees." Next up was Ohio Players, who ran through the cuts "Love Rollercoaster" and "Skin Tight." The headliner, Cameo, seemed like they were on stage for two hours as they delivered hit after hit with "Word Up," "Candy," "Rigamortis" and "Why Have I Lost You." In fact, when they played "Candy," the crowd gathered on the grassy field to do the electric slide, a scene right out of the outro of the film *The Best Man*. I didn't join in—partially because I hadn't mastered the slide hip thrust right before the pivot—but I watched in pride and glee how my people, Black people, communed and moved together with an unspoken, shared signal that was Cameo's staccato guitar strikes in the intro of "Candy."

I knew where I was going to be damn near every Monday every July and August. I'd rush out of the Winthrop Avenue 2 Train station, dodging ladies pushing their ICEE carts so that I could get a good place in line. It was so tempting to walk past the Crown Fried Chicken spot every time, though. The smell of fried pizza rolls beckoned me like a Siren calling to Odysseus. For years, I sat through the tedious pleas of elected officials and long-winded preachers to hear acts like Charlie Wilson, Bootsy Collins, The O'Jays, Patti LaBelle and Teena Marie. Every time then borough president Marty Markowitz started talking, you knew the party was imminent. I even enjoyed contemporary acts like Robin Thicke, Keyshia Cole and Ruben Studdard. It was at Wingate where I first recognized the aroma of marijuana in the air and marveled at the sight of 50- and 60-year-old grandmothers wearing all-denim short sets, displaying their neck and thigh tattoos with pride.

But Mondays weren't good enough. Thursday nights, there were free concerts near Coney Island. With the R&B, funk and Caribbean artists strategically located at Wingate, the pop artists were at Brighton Beach/Coney Island. There, I got to sit in the white seats (if I got there early enough) to watch acts like Huey Lewis & the News, Hall and Oates, John Legend and Gladys Knight. Once again, Markowitz got the party going.

But as much as I loved seeing these amazing legends for free, I was almost as excited to walk over to what was then Astroworld—now Luna Park—to spend a short time partaking in Coney Island activity. I bumped my ass off at El Dorado, a cross between bumper cars and night clubbing. Ah, back then it was $4 to get in and only $1 to ride again. I remember hearing Rihanna and Jay-Z's "Umbrella" on those bumper cars, blasting through DJ-quality speakers and club strobe lights. It was majestic. I made sure not to leave without getting a funnel cake, a Nathan's hot dog or some goodies from Williams Candy Store. Those train rides to Coney Island were brutal, so I had to make sure I took my time while I was out there.

Then there's Celebrate Brooklyn!, the annual performing arts festival at Prospect Park's bandshell. The first time I went was days before I got a new job at BRIC Arts Media, the arts and cultural center that produced Celebrate Brooklyn!. Every time I walked out of the 7th Avenue F train station, I took a quick detour to Uncle Louie G's to get some birthday cake ice cream that was so addictive, I swear to this day it was laced with opioids. The ice cream made that steep walk up 9th Street to Prospect Park bearable on hot, humid days, and the promise of amazing live music kept me focused.

On June 8, 2008, I watched Isaac Hayes's opening night for what turned out to be one of his last concerts before his death. My CitiStorage co-workers and I sat on the grass with blankets and white wine smuggled in via a plastic two-liter bottle of Sprite. I watched the Stax legend sit at a keyboard singing "Don't Let Go," "Joy" and "A Few More Kisses." I was enjoying these classic tunes as the majority white audience was biding their time to hear "Theme from Shaft," the closing tune. Hayes didn't disappoint, and after years of seeing him perform this live on TV, being in his presence was special, not just because of him but because it signaled a new chapter in my professional and personal life that was about to start.

From performances by The Roots, Chaka Khan, Janelle Monae, Gary Clark Jr. and Ari Lennox to film screenings of *Purple Rain* and *Enter the Dragon*, summer nights at Celebrate Brooklyn! were always magically mixed. Monday nights at Wingate Field, I was surrounded by my people. Friendly whites sat with me Thursday nights at the Brighton Beach/Coney Island shows. At Celebrate Brooklyn!, all of Brooklyn was in the park. Suburban moms and their baby strollers and yoga mats sat on the lawn next to young brothers with 3x white T-shirts and Jordan 11 Concords watching WizKid sing "Essence" on the bandshell. What a sight. Only music can do that. Only Brooklyn can do that. ∎

Matthew Allen is a Brooklyn-based TV producer, director and award-winning music journalist. He's written for publications such as Ebony *and interviewed legends like Quincy Jones and Smokey Robinson, while covering concerts by Kendrick Lamar and Janet Jackson. He is currently writing his first book about the history of the Neo-Soul subgenre and is the founder of the DEF|Y|NE Media Substack page.*

Art & Design

Growing up beside a borough that commanded so much attention, Brooklyn cultivated a fiercely independent spirit epitomized by artists like Basquiat and architectural marvels like the Brooklyn Bridge. As the new millennium dawned, a fresh wave of young creatives emerged in Brooklyn, awakening the world to its ever-thriving artistic spirit

Beneath iconic bridges, DUMBO's industrial past fuels a vibrant present with galleries and studios taking over the factory warehouses. Wander cobblestone streets to discover public art like the *DUMBO Walls*. Immerse yourself in the scene with opening night receptions and outdoor exhibits like the *Projection Project*. Engage in special events like First Thursdays gallery nights and the annual *DUMBO Open Studios* (pictured), offering glimpses into creative spaces. Historic architecture, bridge views and restaurants add to the charm of this compact waterfront neighborhood. Find a full event calendar on the Art in DUMBO website. ■

Various, artindumbo.com

Art and Design

Designed to Challenge

The borough is home to world-class museums, but get a better sense of Brooklyn by exploring its idiosyncratic side, where creative expression includes illumination, sonic design and large street murals that once landed artists in jail

Transmitter ignites raw, experimental energy in post-industrial Brooklyn. Founded by six artists in 2014, this dynamic space is an incubator for boundary-breaking art. From immersive environments that envelop the senses to sonic explorations that manipulate sound, *Transmitter* proudly pushes the creative limits of mixed media. A haven for the avant-garde, the gallery provides an atmosphere charged with intellectual curiosity and an aversion to artistic norms. Sharing its building with the equally bold *Tiger Strikes Asteroid*, the space offers a supportive community for off-beat creatives to engage, express and inspire. ■

Transmitter, 1329 Willoughby Avenue, #2A, Bushwick, transmitter.nyc

Home Stylist

Rules are meant to be broken—or at least reimagined. That's the attitude behind *BEAM*, a design store, studio and firm that describes itself as midcentury swagger meets rock 'n' roll. That's the creative vibe. BEAM isn't trying to dictate your style, it wants to elevate it with a playful approach that helps clients express their individuality. In this way, BEAM's mix of furniture, lighting and accessories caters to all tastes, with a handpicked collection of established brands, emerging talent, modern treasures, vintage finds and even the wonderfully weird. ◼

BEAM, 272 Kent Avenue, Williamsburg, beambk.com

From Crime to Canvas

Forty years after New York's mayor declared war on graffiti, the city embraced its long-time foe with the *Bushwick Collective*, a nonprofit that curates street art in the heart of Bushwick. Since the inaugural walls in 2012, artists from around the world have helped transform the neighborhood into a vibrant canvas of creativity. Most murals are temporary, and artists aren't paid, but nabbing wall space is a coveted opportunity that's celebrated each spring with a block party. As a public space, the outdoor gallery is always open and free. ◼

Bushwick Collective, Troutman Street and St. Nicholas Avenue, Bushwick, thebushwickcollective.com

Art School Spirit

Aspiring artists have an ally in *Amant*, a nonprofit started by art collector Lonti Ebers. The multi-venue complex fuels creative exploration and dialogue through exhibitions, education and artist residencies. Designed by the acclaimed SO-IL architects, the 21,000-square-foot campus blends textured concrete and intricate brickwork across several interconnected courtyards and buildings, which house art studios, communal areas, performance spaces and a café. From the Latin word for "they love," Amant also champions art discovery with galleries and events that are always free to the public. ◼

Amant, 315 Maujer Street, East Williamsburg, amant.org

Beau Stanton, Artist

Composing the Chaos

Beau Stanton
A versatile artist known for his large-scale murals, Beau has transformed surfaces across nearly 20 countries. His public art has graced iconic locations from the Berlin Wall and World Trade Center to the famed concrete canvases of the Wynwood Walls and Bushwick Collective

Beau Stanton's murals and artwork vividly color the New York City landscape. From his Red Hook studio, he discusses the local scene, his artistic style and where to find his work in Brooklyn, unintentionally mapping out an epic itinerary for an art walk/bar crawl combo

How do you characterize your artistic style?

Most of the art I produce is in the public, typically large-scale murals, and the visual language could be described as contemporary figurative surrealism. It's about finding little things I appreciate, like historical references, and layering them together to recontextualize the past in a contemporary way.

How do you see visual art as a form of storytelling?

I present visual touchstones that people might have associations with already and then combine them together in one picture. I might have an idea of what that means, but it doesn't mean anyone else will come to the same conclusion, which is the magic. People can pick up on threads of my idea, but I like to present these things in a slightly ambiguous way so there can be a more personal connection with the artwork.

What compelled you to move from Southern California to Brooklyn?

To pursue a career in art, really. I knew I needed to get away from the place I grew up because that's a healthy part of growth, right? I originally wanted to move to Europe because that is where all the stuff I studied happened—beautiful architecture, so close together, so dense—but then I visited New York for the first time on spring break. I had already traveled in Europe, but New York really hit me. It felt familiar, it's closer, and it has a lot of the qualities that I like about Europe. I made the plan to move here as soon as I finished art school.

You were one of the original artists in the Bushwick Collective. What did that mean for you?

The *Bushwick Collective* was a major landmark in the borough, and I still have a piece there. I've had this current wall for 10 years, and before that, I had another wall for four years. They typically turn them around pretty frequently, but I've had this current wall for so long because I was commissioned by the guy who owns the building.

Do you have other murals up in Brooklyn right now?

I have a piece in Red Hook that depicts this really cool ship that was half sunk when I arrived here in 2008. It was a mobile lighthouse—there used to be hundreds of them on the East Coast at one point—parked in one of the inlets in Red Hook. Over time, the boat took on water, and it sank over the course of a decade. When I got the chance to paint this wall, I designed the mural so you could see the whole ship while the gate was open, but when it's closed, you can only see the top of the two masts like the boat in the water. It's on Wolcott Street between Van Brunt Street and Conover. The mural appears in an entire scene of the TV series *Fleishman Is in Trouble*, which was fun.

Brooklyn went through a lot of creative changes in the last 20 years. How would you describe the art scene now compared to when you first arrived?

It felt a lot smaller, and everyone was going to the same art openings. Now it's really expanded out with a lot of galleries in Brooklyn, and the scene feels a lot more fragmented.

For art in general, is there any place you recommend in Brooklyn?

Bushwick Collective, of course, which gets bigger every year. There's another ongoing mural program called *DUMBO Walls*. Shepard Fairey and MOMO had murals there.

One of Beau's murals graces Ra Ra Rhino—sneak in through the photobooth at Lacey Burger to enter

Where do you go in Brooklyn if you want to be out in nature?

This time of year I go to the *Brooklyn Botanic Garden* a lot. You can go every day for two straight months, and it'll be different every day because of the rapid changes in what's blossoming. I take a lot of reference photos for paintings when I go there.

Let's say you're working late on art and want to grab a bite to eat at three in the morning. Where do you go?

Red Hook is great for a lot of things, but late-night food is not one of them. It's mostly an industrial zone, and then my apartment is in Carroll Gardens, which is stroller central, so not too many late-night places either. There is a Yemeni place a lot of taxi cab drivers go to on Atlantic Avenue [in Cobble Hill] called *Hadramout* that I've hit up at night, and it's pretty cool.

Do you have a favorite bar in Brooklyn?

Sunny's is a legendary space that opened as a longshoreman bar when Red Hook was the busiest shipping port in the world. It's more than 100 years old. About a decade ago, they took down some wallpaper and found these beautiful old nautical murals that you can see if you go there.

I also have a newer bar I like called the *Sunken Harbor Club*. I am a little biased because I had a role in the design of the back bar. It's a stained-glass window that looks like the back of a ship, and I have a big painting behind the bar that depicts a mermaid who retook the domain. The ceiling, wood paneling, shelves and hanging lights are all off-kilter to give the illusion of the space being sunk and askew. It's a themed space, like a clubhouse for the survivors of a lost island colony. It's a unique take on a tiki bar.

The bar is new, but the restaurant part is very old. *Gage & Tollner* opened as the first fine-dining restaurant in Brooklyn about 150 years ago. The interior became a designated landmark in 1975. It was the third-ever interior in the whole city to receive landmark status and the first in Brooklyn.

Any paintings in other bars?

I also have a painting in a Bushwick speakeasy called *Ra Ra Rhino*. You enter through a photo booth in *Lacey Burger*. It was a donut shop at the time when I created the piece.

Do you have a local design store you love?

Erie Basin in Red Hook. The guy goes to a lot of estate sales around the Northeast and the Rust Belt, and I have a couple of cool rings from him. I always find very unique stuff in there, like strange ceremonial regalia from the Freemasons or the Odd Fellows.

What advice do you give out-of-town friends when they visit Brooklyn?

Get a bicycle, and the sunsets in Red Hook are the best. The pier is a great place to relax and watch the sun go down over New Jersey, which has some of the most colorful sunsets probably because of the pollution over there.

You've done murals around the world. What tricks have you learned to make long-distance travel easier?

If it's Europe and I'm trying to adapt quickly, I stay up as long as I can when I get there. Otherwise, that deadly thing can happen where you pass out at 5pm and wake up at 2am, and you're screwed. It can be tough to stay awake, but you just have to grind through it. ∎

The Eye of an Era

A photo showcase by Jamel Shabazz

Through Jamel Shabazz's lens, experience Brooklyn life from the eighties to the naughts. A pioneer of street photography, the Red Hook native has produced award-winning works—now in esteemed collections like the Whitney and Smithsonian—that capture personal moments during a new era of self-expression

REAL ESTATE
INSURANCE
FACTORY OUTLET
EVERY DRESS 10
RAY MENS
WIGS
DONUT SHOP
LUNCHEONETTE
WALK
CAMEL

RECORDS VIDEO MOVIES
OFFICIAL
Jewelry
NIKE
1

James Murphy's *The Four Horsemen* is a constant recommendation from Brooklyn locals. Snagging a reservation is tough, so the recommendation is to show up when the kitchen opens (11:00am for lunch, 5:30pm for dinner) to snag a window or bar seat or add your name to the waitlist

Bites

Brooklyn's food scene thrives on the dynamic interplay between its storied past and new culinary frontiers. Wander its streets and breathe it in—the familiar scents of century-old mainstays, authentic aromas from global kitchens, hints of new flavors from pioneering chefs—all woven together on the same table-lined sidewalks

Bridge City Flavors

Forget the melting pot—Brooklyn is a mosaic where food cultures preserve their identities rather than blend them all together. Unlock the true taste of Brooklyn by stepping beyond the familiar and embracing the thrill of exploration

Dough Dynasty

The New York press has heralded a Golden Age of American bakeries, and the golden goodies coming out of Brooklyn ovens are helping make the case. Recent arrival *Welcome Home* brought buzz to Bed-Stuy with signature creations like seasoned ground pork inside lattice croissants, while *Caputo Bakery* has served up Italian classics made in traditional brick ovens for 120 years. Taipei is currently enjoying its own moment of flour power, and *Win Son Bakery* (pictured) brings Taiwanese artistry to Williamsburg with pillowy gems like millet mochi donuts. ∎

Various, see Index, p. 94

Credit: Evan Sung

Night & Day Diner

For nearly a century, the 24-hour *Kellogg's Diner* attracted the city's night owls with its glowing neon sign. It even reached peak cultural cachet when its booths hosted a famous scene between Adam Driver and Lena Dunham in HBO's *Girls*, solidifying its place in the hipster zeitgeist. Now, after a 2024 refresh under new ownership, this Brooklyn landmark is poised for a new era under the neon lights. The Jackie Carnesi–led kitchen brings a tasty blend of Southern comfort, Tex-Mex and crafty cocktails to a classic diner with a new modern style. ■

Kellogg's Diner, 518 Metropolitan Avenue, Williamsburg, kelloggsdinernyc.com

Credits: Julia Gillard

Brooklyn Trattoria

Imagine stepping into a lively Italian trattoria, the kind whispered about by discerning locals in Milan and Bologna. That's the experience ready to embrace you at *Roman's*. Housed inside a vintage-chic space, this seasonal Italian restaurant champions local produce, elegant wines and the simple perfection of freshly made pasta. Roman's first introduced its honest flavors in 2009, with Hannah Shizgal-Paris taking the reins in 2023 after her tenure as head chef at Gjelina NY. As a sibling of She Wolf Bakery, the restaurant enjoys privileged access to its artisan breads, a farmers-market favorite. ■

243 Dekalb Avenue, Fort Greene, romansnyc.com

Brooklyn is the pizza capital of NYC—maybe the world—but with so many choices, where to begin? Your journey starts with a choice: time-honored tradition or daring innovation. For modern marvels, *L'Industrie* (pictured) serves Neapolitan pies with perfectly blistered crusts, while the wood-fired creations at *Paulie Gee's* will blow your mind with toppings like tangy pickled pineapple. Craving authentic classics? Make a pilgrimage to *Luigi's* or *Bay Ridge Pizza*, where generations of expertise shine in every slice. Just remember the local etiquette: always fold your thin-crust slices and leave the utensils behind. ■

Various, see Index, p. 94

Neighborhood Noodles

In a borough bursting with Italian flavor, Williamsburg stands out as a pasta paradise. Missy Robbins, a James Beard winner for NYC's Best Chef, shows why she's a true pasta boss at her two sister restaurants. Her first solo venture, *Lilia*, delivers rustic charm, wood-fired heat and signature dishes like mafaldini with pink peppercorn, while *Misi* goes all-in on noodles, including a glassed-in workshop for watching pasta-makers in action. Prefer something old school? *Bamonte's* has kept it real with red-sauce classics and vintage decor since 1900. ■

Various, Williamsburg, see Index, p. 94

Credit: Rachael Lombardy

Rotisserie Riot

Don't be fooled by the drinks-dominant menu at *The Fly*—the limited food options are by design. This self-proclaimed "chicken bar" stays focused on what it does best: the most delicious rotisserie chicken in town. Fresh off the spit, their free-range New York birds emerge with crackling golden skin that gives way to juicy meat, while the pulled chicken sandwich has achieved cult status among Brooklyn's culinary cognoscenti. A large central bar anchors the room, offering bespoke beverages like craft beer, New York absinthe and lots of natural wine. ■

The Fly, 549 Classon Avenue, Bed-Stuy, theflybrooklyn.com

Many celebrities try their hand at the hospitality game, but James Murphy of LCD Soundsystem stands alone in guiding his restaurant to a Michelin star *and* a James Beard Award. The Grammy winner opened *The Four Horsemen* in 2015 with a dream team of culinary talent, including his business-savvy wife, a Noma-forged chef and a pioneer of the natural wine scene. Over the next decade, Murphy turned the eBay-furnished space into a farm-to-fork favorite for locals and culinary pilgrims alike. The addition of great music, like most of the wine, only comes naturally. ■

295 Grand Street, Williamsburg, fourhorsemenbk.com

Famous Fat Dave, Food Tour Operator
Culinary Cab

Famous Fat Dave
Dave, a former taxi driver who ate his way through the five boroughs, offers custom eating tours in his vintage Checker cab. Lauded by Anthony Bourdain and called a "legend" on the Cooking Channel, he uncovers hidden culinary treasures that amaze tourists and locals alike

Famous Fat Dave takes pride in connecting people with enduring culinary institutions. As the leading authority on local classics and underground eateries, he imagines a Brooklyn food tour loaded with lamb-fat shawarma, bustling Uzbek markets, Peter Luger–inspired pizza and the best cheesecake you'll ever taste

Credit: Valery Rizzo

58

Tell me about your food tours through New York.

I drove a regular Yellow Cab taxi at night and had this crazy concept to find delicious food by speaking to actual human beings rather than using the internet or apps. People were always very proud, like, "Go this place, tell 'em that Richie sent you, gotta ask for Marie and order this." I did this for my own personal edification, but then I started taking family and friends to get the best things in each neighborhood, and then I started taking the friends of family and family of friends. I was faced with a choice: do I get a real job, or do I eat for a living? I went with eating.

What are the first questions you ask clients to help curate a tour?

Some people are just interested in the food or the history or certain areas. Maybe their grandfather is from the Bronx, and they want to see the old neighborhood. I try to get a sense of what they want, but at the same time, you don't want to predetermine the entire tour. When we're driving past one of the most delicious things you could ever eat and some of the most beautiful people you can ever meet, we shouldn't always stick to our arbitrary theme. You want a bit of adventure.

What is your favorite borough for food?

I am a lover, not a fighter, so I love them all, but if you make me choose, Brooklyn is the best for me and my first-time customers because I have the most relationships there. You have the most humanity there—it's literally the borough with the most people—and it's got the most characters. I actually live in Brooklyn, in Coney Island.

How does Coney Island represent quintessential Brooklyn culture?

You have *Nathan's Famous*, the boardwalk, the roller coaster, the beach—it's where all New Yorkers go to get a sea breeze, to get some sun. Even the Native Americans came here to the Land Without Shadows, in their language, before the Europeans arrived. It's a place where New Yorkers, who are not known for relaxing, go to relax.

What are some dishes people might try if they're doing a Brooklyn tour?

You have your basics—a bagel and a schmear, a slice of pizza, a hot dog in Coney Island—but then there are things Brooklynites love that are not in the public imagination as much. For instance, the roast beef sandwich is as much a part of Brooklyn as a hot dog, bagel or pizza. Historically, you go to the beach at Coney Island or Brighton Beach, and on the way back, you stop to get roast beef.

Where do you go?

I often take people to *Brennan and Carr*, an Irish spot on Nostrand Avenue that only works with the top round of the beef, and they collect this salty, bubbly broth when the meat is cooking. They don't even offer horseradish, just cooked onions and American cheese. You dunk your sandwich in this beefy broth, unhinge your jaw and swallow it whole like a snake.

The food is great, the guys are great, and you feel like you're on a movie set in a different time. It's like that for a lot of places. You walk into Brennan and Carr or *Defonte's Sandwich Shop*, and for all intents and purposes—from the food to the accents to the types of people—you could be 50 years back in time. It's the closest you'll get to time travel.

Is there a new place you discovered recently that really blew you away?

Zoares on Coney Island Avenue. A Libyan Jewish Israeli opened it up a few months ago, and they do a ribeye shawarma layered on the spit as they cook it with lamb fat and all these Libyan Jewish spices. They put it in what they call "crazy pita," where they dredge the pita in egg and bread crumbs and fry it so it has the texture of a schnitzel. Then they add shaved, super-high-end beef and lamb-fat shawarma and mix it with tahini, hummus and whatever else you want. I've been taking my customers there, and everybody flips out about it.

When you do Brooklyn pizza tours, do you visit institutions like Di Fara *or a trendy place in Williamsburg or Bushwick?*

I like to mix it up. I'll do some institutions, some new places and then some interesting twists on pizza. For instance, I take people for *adjaruli*, a Georgian dish made with bread, butter, sulguni cheese—their version of mozzarella—and an egg on top. They put it in a pizza box and call it the best pizza in the world.

I don't do *Di Fara* because it's a big, long line there, but I'll go for a classic New York thin slice at *Luigi's*. For a new New York slice like you might find in Williamsburg, I go to *Lucia* on Avenue X in Sheepshead Bay. The guy's father

Tashkent Supermarket lives beneath the elevated subway tracks at Brighton Beach Station

was a pizza man for 40 years, and he'll make a classic slice but ferment the dough a little more and add some extra virgin olive oil, shaved pecorino and a little fresh basil on top. Lucia is the best of both worlds: old school and new school. He does his father's vodka slice, but he also does a creamed spinach slice inspired by *Peter Luger Steak House*. He does a clam pie on Fridays, a shrimp pie on Saturdays.

If someone wants to stop at a Brooklyn food market, where would you go?

There's an Uzbek market called *Tashkent* that's bustling with not just Uzbeks, but all kinds of people, mostly former Soviets down in Brighton Beach. It has the best-prepared foods you can imagine, like seafood salads, incredible soups, incredible breads, plov, shawarma, but—and this is great for them—they just opened in the West Village. Now I feel I wouldn't take people there because they could just go to the one in the West Village.

Lately, I'll go down to Brooklyn's Chinatown along 8th Avenue. They've got very interesting things,

like rice rolls where they steam the liquefied rice with some meat and egg and then roll it up and add all these sauces. It has this crazy texture.

For cheesecake, is Junior's *still the spot?*

Junior's is the gold standard, but they make it in New Jersey, not Brooklyn, and now they have a location in Times Square. For me, the best cheesecake is at *Villabate Alba* on 18th Avenue in the Little Italy section of Brooklyn. It's been around since 1932.

So there's Jewish cheesecake and Italian cheesecake. The Italian version has a ricotta base, while the Jewish cheesecake—also called New York cheesecake, or what the Italians call American cheesecake—has a cream cheese base. Junior's is great, but it's very dense. The Italians at Villabate Alba managed to make a New York-Jewish-American cheesecake with a cream cheese base that's really light. It's one of those desserts where you take a bite and the muscles in your shoulders just relax and your eyes roll back and all of your problems melt away. ■

With friends at *With Others*. A natural wine bar along Bedford Avenue offering an evening seat and community-feel, glass after glass

Sips

The backdrop may shift—a secret speakeasy, a gritty dive, a rooftop lounge with skyline views—but the spirit of the scene remains the same with inspired takes on modern mixology. From honkytonks like *Skinny Dennis* to caviar martinis at *Maison Premiere*, a new generation of Brooklyn bars, breweries and sommeliers will expand your palate and fuel new stories and connections

Sip & Slurp

A crisp cava or dry Chablis is a traditional match for oysters, but enjoy a martini-oyster pairing to see Brooklyn at its creative best. For elegant French flair, *Le Crocodile* offers classic martinis alongside fresh, briny oysters in a chic setting, while *Deux Chats* (pictured) sets a moodier stage with East Coast oysters, inventive drinks and a 13-glass martini fountain. If it's the first Monday of the month, check out the latest guest martini at *Grand Army Bar* and then challenge your flavor limits with novel oyster toppings like Japanese tsuyu mignonette. ■

Various, see Index, p. 94

Sips

Craft City Pours

From intimate wine bars to energetic taprooms to unexpected martini and oyster pairings, Brooklyn's got your fix. Forget the familiar and go beyond. These are the innovators, pushing boundaries and inviting you to discover something extraordinary

Hops Dreams

Brooklyn's craft beer scene is giving New England a run for its money with buzzworthy spaces across the borough. Women- and veteran-owned *TALEA Beer Co.* (pictured) delights with fruit-forward sours, hazy IPAs and bold creations like a sour ale brewed with mango, tamarind, lime and habanero. Find their craft goodness at two inviting taprooms in Brooklyn as well as retail stores and Michelin-starred restaurants in the state. *Other Half Brewing* is a must for serious hop lovers, with intense double IPAs, sweet pastry stouts and wacky beer names like Space Broccoli and Out for Trout. For a mix of classic staples and inventive twists, head to *Threes Brewing* in Gowanus, whose menu collaboration with Grand Army surely inspired its oyster-shell pilsner. ■

Various, see Index, p. 94

Have Glass Will Travel

Palmetto's drink menu is a passport to flavor with global stops like Jakarta-Colada, Oaxacan Coffee and Torino Pastis. There's even a grown-up Orange Julius slushie for the Carnival Cruise crowd. Natural wines join the journey, from French and Italian estates to emerging growers in Hungary and Georgia, to savor alongside Mediterranean snacks like Marcona almonds and tinned sardines. Add bright decor, lush greenery and vinyl DJs, and Palmetto feels like a tasting tour of backpacker bucket lists, but it still finds a way to retain a friendly neighborhood vibe. ∎

Palmetto, 309 Knickerbocker Avenue, Bushwick, palmettobushwick.com

Monks Gone Wild

Bitter Monk, a new cocktail bar and micro-distillery, crafts elixir spirits with botanicals foraged across New York State. Signature cocktails, often named after creative icons, include the Marie Laveau—a smoky fusion of bourbon, fig leaf and amaro—channeling the mystique of the legendary voodoo queen. Dramatic stained-glass art bathes the space in a colorful glow, illuminating the mixologists in action. An offshoot of Harlem's Sugar Monk, the space doubles as a tasting room for its brand, Atheras Spirits, with an oversized window that peers into its production lab. ∎

Bitter Monk, 68 34th Street, 2nd floor, Sunset Park, bittermonk.com

Williamsburg Uncorked

Imagine a cozy evening in Williamsburg, glass in hand. These wine bars make it a reality. *With Others*, a stylish space with minimalist design, showcases small-batch vineyards with an emphasis on female growers and natural wines. Book early to secure a spot for its Sunday Wine School tastings. Heading east, you'll find a rustic counterpoint in *Tuffet*'s (pictured) exposed brick walls and vintage charm. The bar warmly welcomes freelancers during the day, while the night crowd enjoys wines by the glass, meat and cheese plates, seasonal sangrias and even an outdoor fireplace. ∎

Various, see Index, p. 94

The Brooklyn Mixtress

Julie Reiner
A pioneer of California's craft cocktail movement, Julie ignited the New York scene upon her arrival in the mid-1990s. This bar owner, author and *Drink Masters* judge (Netflix) has won every award and made every list imaginable, keeping Brooklyn at the forefront of global mixology

Craft cocktail icon Julie Reiner helms the award-winning *Clover Club*, but her discerning palate extends beyond boutique bars. With impeccable taste, she navigates the borough's best, from celebrated restaurants and street fairs to dispensaries and parks, including the perfect place to enjoy a haunted Halloween

Tell me about your start in San Francisco.

I started bartending in college at Florida State, but I moved to San Francisco to get a real job. I worked in marketing, and it was really boring, so I went back into hospitality. I really started learning how to bartend at a place called the Red Room, and then I worked at a drag queen restaurant called AsiaSF where the whole back bar was a runway. It was the 1990s in California with fresh ingredients and farm to table. We were using fresh juices in cocktails. Then I met my future wife, who got into grad school at NYU, and I moved across the country with her six months after we met, as you do.

How was your early New York experience?

I got a job at a cocktail bar in the West Village called C3, and I was making my own menus based on what I was doing in San Francisco. Then I started talking to the pastry chef about flavor pairings and making my own syrups and infusions to give people the best thing I could in a glass. Almost overnight, I found myself on the front page of the *New York Times* food section.

Why pastry chefs?

Pastry and mixology are hand in hand; you just stop when it gets to eggs and flour. Back then, you didn't have the tools you have now. There was no flavor bible, no [modern] cocktail books, and you didn't have the internet, not really. I was just trying to bring a culinary approach to cocktails and do things very few people were doing at the time.

What's an example of an early cocktail?

One of my regulars told me about an apple martini he had in Los Angeles, and I wanted to make one. At the time, I didn't know what Apple Pucker was, so I took Granny Smith green apples and soaked them in vodka for a week, and then strained them out and made a martini. It tasted like biting into an apple with a kick.

I ultimately got fired from this bar for doing too good of a job. When people started flocking to the bar, the restaurant wasn't super busy, so it became a walkway to the bar in the back. It really pissed off the chef and the GM.

As someone who had a bar that specialized in Latin spirits, do you have a Latin restaurant you can recommend in the area?

Claro is a Oaxacan restaurant on Third Avenue in Gowanus, and the food is excellent. I don't know if it has a star, but it's in the *Michelin Guide.*

What's your favorite restaurant in Brooklyn that serves a less widely known cuisine?

There's a spot called Matawana that—no, that's a dispensary. It's *Masalawala*, and they specialize in Bengali cuisine. There's also a great Korean restaurant called *Haenyeo* and a Szechuan spot near *The Clover Club* called *Shan.*

Do you have a favorite dispensary?

Yeah, *Matawana*! It's actually great.

What about someone else's bar?

Bar Goto Niban on Bergen Street. It's a Japanese-inspired cocktail bar by Kenta Goto, who used to be our head bartender at Pegu Club back in the day.

Do you have any recommendations for finding good bars in general?

Don't always focus on the "best" bars. There's a lot of BS out there. Find more underground

The Clover Club hosts live jazz each Sunday during brunch

recommendations that aren't based on PR companies pressuring people to include their clients. Sometimes that means getting out of the busy neighborhoods. A lot also depends on what you're looking for—cocktail wise, food, historical spots that have more to offer than just the latest molecular situation.

For me, bars are about people. I can sit at a bar that has the most amazing cocktail, but if the bartender is not very exciting and there's no engagement from the team, I would rather have a negroni at a different bar with a better vibe and where the staff's excited you're there.

Do you have a favorite annual event in Brooklyn?

The Atlantic Antic is always entertaining. It's been happening on Atlantic Avenue for a really long time with all these old-school restaurants. They do barbecued stuff outside, and there are bands. A lot of the street fairs in New York are very generic, like selling the same shit at every single one, but this one is different.

What about a favorite museum or gallery?

The *Brooklyn Museum* is pretty incredible. There are so many great things because Brooklyn is huge. It would be the third-largest city in the US if it wasn't a borough. There's cool art happening in Williamsburg—I went to a Beastie Boys thing there with cool memorabilia—but I don't get to Williamsburg that much because it's not easy to get there from Carroll Gardens. You typically have to go through Manhattan unless you're near the G train.

There are a lot of cultural enclaves across Brooklyn with great restaurants and grocery stores. Do you have any favorites?

I recently moved to Greenwood [Heights], which is on the edge of Sunset Park. The Brooklyn Chinatown there has really cool dim sum and great food. There's also a lot of authentic Mexican and Latin restaurants in the area. This side of Fifth Avenue has Latin grocery stores that are fun to explore.

The Green-Wood Cemetery is beautiful.

The cemetery is stunningly beautiful. I walk by it all the time. It has fountains, hills, little lakes and lots of history. There's something very calming about it. Over Halloween, they do a walking tour of the cemetery at night. It's such a fun thing to do. I know it sounds morbid, but it's a really beautiful park that people just happen to be buried in. We're also close to Prospect Park, which is incredible.

What recommendations do you have for someone coming to Brooklyn for the first time?

It's important to understand how big Brooklyn is and plan accordingly. They might make plans for Williamsburg and Carroll Gardens and not realize how much time it's going to take traveling between the two. Choose neighborhoods that are close together and then figure out what you want to do in each. So if you're in this area where the Clover Club is, you can go to the *Brooklyn Paramount* theater, the Brooklyn Museum, DUMBO and *Gage & Tollner*, which is a very classic old-school restaurant. Choose things within the same vicinity, and then maybe go over to Williamsburg another day and do that area.

Any other recommendations?

Central Park and Rockefeller Center have ice skating rinks in the winter, but you can't even get on there. It's insane. There's an ice skating rink underneath the Brooklyn Bridge, and it's so beautiful. The rink in Prospect Park is amazing, but the one under the Brooklyn Bridge is just this iconic experience, and then you can go to one of the OG pizza joints over there. I mean, there's so much to do in Brooklyn. People who visit New York City can stay in Brooklyn and never even go into Manhattan, and a lot of people do that. ∎

It now has locations across the country, but the original *Brooklyn Bowl* started in its namesake, on Wythe Avenue. Catch the likes of a Dave Matthews tribute band in between frames—literally. There are bowling lanes adjacent to the dance floor

Sounds

Brooklyn has long been a mothership for music—from the Black-owned jazz bars that welcomed Thelonius Monk after his Cabaret Card was revoked to the underground 1970s punk scene to Biggie's freestyling era. Come here for a storied past and sound rooms of many sizes

Spread Love, It's the Brooklyn Way

There's no shortage of noise in New York between subway buskers, stoop saxophonists and the steady hum of street life. Brooklyn maintains its own voice in the mix, attracting both hyperlocal and international acts. These days, every corner has an independent venue, vinyl bar or backyard show we want in on

Real-life Radio

The Lot Radio streams music all day, every day from Greenpoint—making tuning in a tactile experience. It's a platform for local artists in residence and surprise appearances: Jamie xx, Adam Port and Four Tet have come through. In true Brooklyn form, the concept feels like something between a scrappy house party and a nicely groomed parking lot. It's open year-round with a DJ booth and drink hut, but warmer months are the busiest. ∎

The Lot Radio, 17 Nassau Avenue, Greenpoint, thelotradio.com

Credit: Freddy Weber

For the Lunatics

Come for tasty Mediterranean bites, communal seating and live shows at *LunÀtico* in Bed-Stuy. This is a hub for global sounds, where no two acts are the same. Expect a well-traveled crowd that's simultaneously music-obsessed and just looking to immerse themselves in a lively atmosphere. The energy in the room is contagious, so be prepared to fall in love with a new genre every time you come back. Music typically starts at 9pm and 10:15pm nightly with a $10 suggested donation. Arrive early to snag a seat. ∎

LunÀtico, 486 Halsey Street, Bed-Stuy, barlunatico.com

Good Listeners

Date night or just you and tunes, these ones are spot on. The soul-warming *Kissa Kissa* is a Japanese hi-fi jazz bar and record shop with a library of over 5,000 LPs lining its walls. Order the shiso-laced mojito or moorish peaches and cream punch. Then there's dinner and a DJ set at *Eavesdrop* (pictured), a cozy locale designed entirely around sound and serious cocktails. Behind the sorta-secret entrance in *Upside Pizza*, *Ask for Janice* is home to a curated menu of drinks, film screenings and 1990s hip-hop mix tapes. ∎

Various, see Index, p. 94

Sports and a Show

Why do one thing when you could do several at the iconic 16-lane, 23,000-square-foot *Brooklyn Bowl*? Converted from an 1800s ironworks building, this place arguably brought hype to Williamsburg. Sounds from inside can typically be heard down the street, inviting you in for local beer on tap, concerts from artists you know or, yes, bowling. The venue—situated on prime Wythe Avenue—has LEED-certified pin-setters and a stage made of recycled tires. Get rooftop sunset drinks at the *Wythe Hotel*'s *Bar Blondeau* before posting up here. ■

Various, see Index p. 94

Dawn Patrol

You might not need coffee if you've got tickets to *Daybreaker*, a morning party that's over a decade deep and still dancing. Headquartered near McCarren Park, what started as a social experiment to socialize sans booze has become a worldwide collective of people willing to roll out of bed and rave. Drop by to move, drip in the sauna at select events or surrender to caffeine among the like-minded. If you're even a little curious, book it before spots sell out. ■

Daybreaker, various locations, daybreaker.com

Quirky Türkiye

Head out for nightlife in the back of Bushwick's eccentric *The Turk's Inn*, a replica of a legendary Wisconsin supper club that once served movers and shakers Silk Road fare. Decor in *The Sultan Room* is equally impeccable, with moody lighting and plenty of nooks to tuck yourself away in. Album releases and events are always happening here, so get your friends on the list before the club reaches its 201-person capacity. Available for private bookings. ■

Various, see Index, p. 94

Eli Escobar, DJ

Soaked in Sounds

Eli Escobar
Eli is a New York–born DJ and owner of *Gabriela*, an intimate nightclub in Williamsburg that prioritizes local talent over big-name lineups, where he runs the decks on Thursday evenings. He's also played his vocal-forward sets at Brooklyn hotspots like The *Lot Radio* and *Paragon*

The pulse of Brooklyn beats in Eli's veins, a rhythm echoed in his DJ sets. A constant presence in the borough's nocturnal scene, his sound is a love letter to the city's creative energy. He shares the genesis of his craft, reflects on the innovative power Brooklyn holds, and muses about *Gabriela*, where sound takes flight

Gabriela
Williamsburg

Tell us a little bit about your background as a DJ. What got you started in the industry?

I was going out clubbing in high school and got a bit obsessed with the idea of being the person in the club who controlled what everyone was listening to. I felt like "Okay, I think I could do that." I was given a pair of hand-me-down turntables from a friend after graduating high school, and I already had a record collection because I'd been collecting records since I was super young. I just started messing with it and I got the bug. I was feverishly collecting records and just trying to make sure I had everything and every genre; I wanted to be able to play everything. After college, I jumped into the scene and started DJing all the time.

How has the Brooklyn music scene influenced your taste or style?

After playing clubs in Manhattan for so long, when nightlife exploded in Brooklyn—not that it wasn't happening before, but I mean the dawn of the new electronic music scene as we know it now in Brooklyn— it felt very open. It felt like, "Wow, I can just play all the music I want to play and everybody here is into it and dancing?" It was a really inspiring moment and a shift in the way I was able to play.

Are there any favorite historical musical figures from Brooklyn who influence your music?

When I was interested in DJing back in high school, my main love was hip-hop—I know you think I'm gonna say Biggie; I'm not gonna say Biggie. The definitive Brooklyn rapper at the time for me was Big Daddy Kane. Big Daddy Kane was first and he had a very unique style, his wordplay, the way he dressed— all of it was very "Okay, that's Brooklyn." He really epitomized

what I thought of Brooklyn at the time; it was different than Queens, it was different than Long Island, different than Harlem.

When you hear me DJ now, you might not be like "Wow, he must have been influenced by Big Daddy Kane," but that was New York back then. We all soaked it in.

Do you have any muses here in Brooklyn?

It's gonna be really corny, but I feel like my muse has always just been the city. I don't mean Manhattan, I mean New York City. When I feel inspired is when I'm going across the bridge and I just see the buildings, or playing music on a rooftop with a sick view, or just walking down the street. That's always informing the music I make and how I'm gonna play that day or that night.

One of the things that I was really intentional about when we opened *Gabriela* was not falling into the trap of needing to book big headlining DJs and have lineups every night. I just wanted it to be a place where local DJs could play all night long—on their own or back-to-back with one other person— and the people who are coming here would trust that the music is always consistent; it doesn't matter if the DJ playing is a huge draw.

What's your mindset like when you're in the studio versus at a live set?

When I make music, it's really like a thing that I only do when I feel a need for it. I don't plan it. I'm not one of those people who's like, gotta go to the studio and try to work. I only make music when I have an idea or it feels right.

When I'm DJing, I know I'm playing three or four nights a week, start time, end time. Almost without fail, I really look forward to it. It's a bit of a therapeutic thing for

On Thursday evenings, Eli plays to a smokey crowd of music lovers and late-nighters at Gabriela

me. I haven't lost any passion for it at all.

Do you prefer playing to a big audience or a low-key smaller crowd?

Always low-key, no doubt about it. The main thing that can be tough about big crowds is the separation. When we do Cheeky Disco, we're really close to the crowd, so it's great. I can see everyone's faces. I can see if they're happy. That's the most important thing to me. And usually, the sound is better.

Have you ever heard a sound in the street and put it in a mix?

I have in my albums, lots of times. Kids playing at a playground, cars—I've done it so many times. If I'm coming up with an idea in my head while walking down the street, musically, then when I put it down and add a little bit of background

noise, it feels true to the moment when I came up with the music.

What's the most underrated Brooklyn neighborhood to spend time in?

I really love Sheepshead Bay. Underrated to I don't know whom, but I would recommend everyone spend some time there, eat some seafood. It's the best; I love it there.

After a set in Brooklyn, where are you going out?

After I'm done playing I'm usually going home, but I used to head to *Wo Hop.*

What are some of the best places you'd recommend that someone visiting Brooklyn go to? Food, shops, art?

What's the name of the really famous museum? *Brooklyn Museum.* Never misses. It's a beautiful space. For food I would strongly

Café Mogador
Williamsburg

Bunna Cafe
Bushwick

recommend *Café Mogador* on Wythe Avenue. It's a family-owned Moroccan restaurant, originally opened in the East Village in the eighties.

If you want to try really good Ethiopian food, I would suggest *Bunna Cafe* in Bushwick; it's vegan.

Also, come to *Gabriela* if you like music and being around awesome people—one of the best sound systems in the city.

What makes Brooklyn special?

I grew up here, and what makes it special is the mix of people. The cultures—the immigrants, the people who were born here, everything we all bring to this city to make it what it is. You have these communities who might seem like they keep to themselves, but when push comes to shove, we all look out for each other here. ■

Startups

Brooklyn's new creative vanguard is not just making things, but rewriting possibilities. Luxury spaces are sourcing floral arrangements born of Bushwick's surreal dreams. An insider's content creator hub comes to life in a once-dormant Greenpoint factory, while the borough's star media brand redefines itself to tell the sturdiest borough's story

New Brooklyn Rulebreakers

There's a new creative pulse growing in Brooklyn, from Molly Ford's wild florals to Graza's bold olive oil. The Lighthouse creator campus sparks collabs, and BKMAG elevates local culture. Unapologetically Brooklyn, these innovators rewrite the rules with grit and vision

Afford the Squeeze

Brooklyn-born Andrew Benin set out to make world-class olive oil without the pretentious price tag. *Graza* would be bold, flavorful and, above all, squeezable. The playbook was simple: get chefs hooked first, then let word of mouth do the rest. Sourced from Spanish groves, Williamsburg-based *Graza* keeps it affordable without cutting corners. No fancy pedigree, just grit, good oil and a vibe as real as a Bushwick warehouse party. Now it's on shelves from Whole Foods to Target and in Michelin-starred kitchens. It proves that everyone, not just fancy restaurants, wants great oil. ∎

Graza Olive Oil, @getgraza

Nestled in the old Eberhard Faber Pencil Factory, *The Lighthouse* is different from the typical Brooklyn co-working space. This Greenpoint creative hub blends their 19th-century industrial bones with Brooklyn's maker spirit, offering perks like expert-led lunch-and-learns. The Lighthouse's first outpost in Venice Beach recently hosted Slow Ventures' $60M Creator Fund and an exclusive preview of Will Smith's album, but here, it's going to be totally Brooklyn-focused. Surrounded by indie shops, vinyl bars and pierogi spots, it's where next-level connections are made. No generic co-working—just fuel for Brooklyn's next big ideas. ∎
The Lighthouse, @thelighthousecampus

Florals, Interrupted

Molly Ford didn't just want to arrange flowers, she wanted to rewrite the rules of New York floristry. Her garden arrangements with *Flowers by Ford* have graced the New York Botanical Garden's Orchid Dinner at The Plaza Hotel and brought wild elegance to arrangements for jeweler Mejuri. Based in her Bushwick studio, she blends foraged textures with curated blooms from the New York Street Market, creating pieces that feel freshly plucked from her dreams. Ford's recent use of calla lilies inspired by Diego Rivera's paintings captures her vibe petal by petal. ∎
Molly Ford, @flowersbyford

BK on Brooklyn

For nearly 15 years, *BKMAG* (formerly *Brooklyn Magazine*) has been an insider's guide to the best in culture, entertainment and food, brought to you with deep cultural insight. Recently backed by BSE Global—owners of the Brooklyn Nets—they onboarded editors Lucas Wisenthal and Michael Gonik to helm the institution. Together, they're doubling down on what makes Brooklyn tick, from underground artists to local politics. Check out their evolved socials to see a new side of Brooklyn's story. Whether you live here or just love it, *BKMAG* is your hype man for everything Brooklyn. ∎
BKMAG, @brooklynmagazine

Point-n-Shoot Culture

These Brooklyn content creators figured out how to succeed at monetizing social media, and it's all gravy. They blend the immigrant experience, unheralded voices and a dash of history for an irresistible slice of culture

Foodie Journo

Jeremy Jacobowitz isn't just a sandwich fanatic—he's a culinary storyteller who turned his passion into a global brand with 500K+ Instagram followers. Brooklyn-bred, the ex–Good Morning America producer went viral analyzing NYC's best bread and never stopped. Whether launching the Brunch Boys or taste-testing 100+ sandwiches in one reel, he blends journalism, humor and "carb devotion," making food an adventure. His Substack dishes on the city's hidden dining gems—from tucked-away bodegas to midnight dumpling joints—and why the perfect bite should always be messy. As a trusted LOST iN ambassador and contributor, he guides viewers through the best eats beyond the borough in the likes of Tokyo, Venice Beach, Bologna and beyond. ■

Jeremy Jacobowitz, @jeremyjacobowitz

Brooklyn Beyond Bushwick

Lauren Riley and Merlyn Oliver, the Brooklyn Mavens, spotlight the borough's diverse culture. Raised in Prospect Heights and East Flatbush, they highlight hidden gems—from Black-owned bakeries to forgotten jazz landmarks. With 70,000+ Instagram followers, they've been featured in *Time Out* for celebrating Brooklyn's diversity beyond what's new and trendy in Williamsburg and Bushwick. The Mavens blend history and humor in their popular walking tours. Their work with local historians and NYC Tourism, and their own viral posts on Brooklyn's Black heritage, cements their status as the borough's most authentic guides. ■

The Brooklyn Mavens, @bklynmavens

Immigrant Food Legacy

Angela Xu, aka the Brooklyn Food Lady, serves up an eclectic blend of food photography and storytelling that celebrates immigrant communities and local culture. Her collaborations with mom-and-pop eateries spotlight underrepresented voices, while her Substack dives into the history of iconic but shuttered restaurants like Dubrow's Cafeteria. Angela's passion shines in her explorations of Brooklyn neighborhoods, where she uncovers the stories behind internationally inspired local cuisines. The Brooklyn Food Lady feed feels less like a showcase and more like an invitation to savor the connections food creates across people and decades. ■

Angela Xu, @brooklynfoodlady

Noah Chaimberg and Allison Zuckerman,
Business Owner and Artist

Art & Hot Sauce

Noah Chaimberg and
Allison Zuckerman
Noah Chaimberg founded
cult-favorite hot sauce brand
Heatonist after doing years of
pop-ups. Allison Zuckerman's
vibrant paintings have been
featured in Chelsea galleries
and on Brooklyn murals. They
live in Greenpoint, and their
new baby will likely inherit
both a tolerance to spicy food
and a paintbrush

Greenpoint fuels Noah and Allison's creativity. Its grit inspires his boundary-pushing hot sauces and her bold paintings. The couple tells us where to see the best art in Bushwick, where to find the spiciest bites, and why you should always take the NYC ferry

Tell me about your Brooklyn meet-cute.

Noah: We technically met in the elevator of the building that we lived in. We had matched on Hinge, and it just happened that I was moving that week into the building where Allison already lived.

Allison: So he was stalking me.

Noah: And then on the way to our first date, I said, "Do you want to go and we'll walk over there together?" And she said, "No, I'll meet you there." So I figured that she was going to stand me up.

Allison: I wanted to get in the zone and listen to some music. Collect my thoughts up to the last second.

Noah: But then I was on the way down to the lobby to head out and walk over there, and the elevator door opened on Allison's floor, and there she was.

Allison, does Noah inspire your artwork?

Allison: I think definitely the support is there, and it's inspiring to have that kind of belief in my vision and what I'm doing because painting is a complicated field to be in. Just having that belief in me is very inspiring. And we have great conversations. I'll come up with an idea, talk to Noah about it, and we flesh it out. That can be pretty exciting too. I wouldn't say, "Oh, I'm inspired by hot sauce, and I'm gonna make a painting about it." I haven't gotten to that point yet.

Does Allison inspire your hot sauce creations, Noah?

Noah: I think there's a lot that Allison does with artwork that has bled through into what I do, especially about mixing genres and pulling from different eras and elements. The thought process is a big part of Allison's work, and I think

it's something we do a lot more with my work too—looking at different cuisines or types of food. Like, what's the difference between a buffalo sauce and a hot sauce? How do we blur these lines and pull relevant elements from different things to create something new?

Do you have a shared Brooklyn neighborhood that you love?

Noah: We live in Greenpoint and love it. It's more neighborhood-y than South Williamsburg, where we met. Greenpoint has *Radio Bakery*—people wait hours for croissants, even in winter. It got a ton of press as being one of the best bakeries in New York, so every weekend, there's a line that goes down half a block. People seem happy they're waiting out in the sunshine or snow for an hour-plus for a croissant.

Allison, has Brooklyn inspired any of your projects?

Allison: I've done two murals with Colossal Media. One represented Brooklyn for a female-run champagne company, incorporating iconic Brooklyn imagery. The other was for TikTok's Jewish American Pride History Month. Both were amazing experiences, though the murals are now painted over.

What's the artists' world in Brooklyn like for you?

Allison: My studio's in Bushwick; there's a great art community there. My building has DJs, photographers, tattoo artists. Sometimes I run into a grad school friend in the elevator, and we do impromptu studio visits. I mostly show in Chelsea or the Lower East Side, but Brooklyn's inspiring. My work became maximalist here. Everything's in your face; there's no distance in the urban context.

Noah, your website says you're a "hot sauce sommelier." What is that exactly?

Allison: It makes sense to call him that. Noah's always recommending pairings. We're going to see my family tomorrow, and we're bringing hot sauce. Noah's already thinking about what'll go well with what my mom is preparing. There's definitely something to it. I think certain hot sauces can take a culinary dish to the next level.

Noah: Totally. Nobody eats hot sauce by itself, it's always going on something, so pairing is important. It's not so much what I do anymore, though. When we started the company a dozen years ago, we were a retailer sourcing craft makers worldwide, so pairing was key. Now, we mostly make hot sauces. Learning about ingredients, getting influences from different cuisines and creating new stuff.

Let's go back to when you started 1 2 years ago.

Noah: When I started, it was a passion project where I sold hot sauce from a pushcart at Brooklyn markets. I loved hot sauce and wanted a creative outlet, so I made a brand. I had a full-time corporate job in Midtown Monday to Friday, then weekends pushing the cart. People loved it. They'd say, "I didn't know hot sauce could be like this!" They'd think of vinegar and chili peppers, Tabasco, maybe sriracha. Showing them blueberry hot sauce or Szechuan peppercorns expanded their idea of what it could be.

For both of you, what's the biggest difficulty of doing business in Brooklyn, and how do you make it work?

Allison: Expenses. My studio rent keeps going up—no sink, but the price of a one-bedroom apartment.

Noah: Logistics are complicated. Pickups, deliveries, even trash removal is a hassle. Everything requires coordination and can be a hassle compared to the suburbs.

Where do you like to see art in Brooklyn?

Allison: I really enjoy the murals that we see around Bushwick where I work. Some of them are very inspiring too. I think they really add a lot of personality to the neighborhood. Then in Greenpoint there's *Open Studios* that happens I think two or three times a year, where they'll put out a map and all the artists that have studios in this neighborhood will open up their doors to everyone for an afternoon.

Noah, are there any Brooklyn hot sauce makers you partner with?

Noah: There's a great scene here. Queen Majesty is a hot sauce maker who's been doing it in New York for as long as I have. There's a big community of hot sauce makers here, which is fun, because when we throw an event we'll all invite each other so you see each other out socially too. We all collaborate and socialize at events like the NYC Hot Sauce Expo.

Allison, do you enjoy hot sauce? Any favorite dishes or restaurants?

Allison: I do enjoy hot sauce, though Noah has expanded my world of it. I like a nearby Thai restaurant, *Chinta Thai*, for spicy food. Noah also makes an "Everything Bagel" hot sauce with ghost pepper powder that I love.

Do you have any tips for people who love hot sauce but deal with acid reflux?

Noah: I recommend mild sauces and listening to your body. We have

Allison's mural was on view the summer of 2024 on Waterbury Street in Bushwick

a mild line called Hot Ones Junior for kids. Eating something like a banana before spicy food can help reduce acid reflux. It's important not to push yourself too hard.

Allison: It's actually something that I've been dealing with through my pregnancy. Now I have a lot of heartburn, but I'm not giving up the hot sauce, so I'm drinking a ton of milk and Tums are my best friend.

Both of you just returned from a trip to Italy, so we have to know your best travel advice.

Noah: If you're in NYC, take the ferry to and from Brooklyn. It's a beautiful boat ride and a great way to see the city and stay connected to nature. It's a beautiful way to see the city.

Allison: When traveling internationally, focus on food and exploring by walking and snacking. Don't overplan. Enjoy sitting outside, people-watching and discovering places spontaneously. ∎

A Buchanan's mural painted by Colossal Media

Brooklyn Walldogs Bite into Branding

Brooklyn's artistic spirit, always too big to be contained by galleries alone, has animated its public spaces for decades. This legacy has inspired a new wave of street art: hand-painted mural campaigns that fit seamlessly into the borough's colorful streetscape. The sheer scale and artistry of these murals—some soaring six stories high—will compel any urban explorer to pause for a moment of appreciation.

These works are the signature of Colossal Media, the force that revitalized hand-painted advertising in Brooklyn and beyond. Its vision is to orchestrate unique, real-world engagements where every wall tells a story and every brushstroke celebrates the streets.

Launched from a Park Slope garage more than 20 years ago, Colossal bridges the gap between street culture and lifestyle branding. Its large-scale murals function as public art, offering a tangible, textured counterpoint to the fleeting gloss of digital displays and vinyl billboards. In a media world driven by online impressions, murals inspire offline interactions that bond with the public in ways that clickbait can't. Hand-painted works resonate more deeply, from their blue-collar nature to their roots in local street culture, and even their creation serves as a form of performance art. In an ironic twist, public art also thrives on social media, allowing the murals to spread across the digital realm in an organic way.

Still, Colossal canvases are more than large-scale contrasts to small-screen marketing. Creating an elaborate piece might be time-consuming and physically demanding, but it can help shape neighborhood aesthetics and foster genuine community connection. To uphold this standard, Colossal is deliberate in its partnerships and production. This includes using 1 Shot paint and Ronan paints—another nod to sign painting, New York's hand-painted advertising tradition and street culture—chosen for their exceptionally bright and durable colors.

Even if your Brooklyn adventure just started, chances are you've already seen a Colossal canvas. Perhaps you recall the Brat Wall, the dynamic, live-streamed mural in Brooklyn celebrating Charli XCX's album launch? That was a Colossal project. Or maybe you know SoHo's iconic Gucci Art Wall, a rotating canvas recognized as a Google Maps landmark? Also Colossal. You may have even seen their work in your home state. Their signature murals now grace walls across the country in cities like Atlanta, Los Angeles, Portland, Chicago, Nashville, Austin and San Francisco.

Headquartered in Williamsburg, the company claims its highest concentration of murals in Brooklyn. Around 70 of their wallscapes adorn corridors like Bedford Avenue, Wythe Avenue and Kent Avenue, but commercial projects are only part of the picture. Colossal launched its Start Today initiative for community outreach, with pro bono projects like the "You Are Not Alone" mural to address mental health stigma. They also champion local talent, once turning a high schooler's Scholastic Award–winning photo into a four-story mural that an NBC correspondent dubbed the "Mona Lisa of Williamsburg."

Inclusivity is another company value, with Colossal challenging male dominance in street art. Led by President Kelly Peppers and featuring accomplished painters like Janine Taylor—the first Colossal-trained woman painter to rank up from apprentice to expert painter—the company disrupts gender expectations across operations.

"As a woman in a male-dominated field, our presence not only adds diversity but also enriches the dialogue, creating a more inclusive work environment," Taylor shares. "Embracing diverse perspectives elevates our craft and empowers the changing face of walldogs."

The company's commitment to inclusivity includes a paid apprenticeship program for aspiring "walldogs," the trade's affectionate name for outdoor advertising mural painters, that broadens opportunities for creatives of all types. Colossal takes on new apprentices based on projected need, and the experience gives future walldogs a pathway to turn their talents into a possible career. Further supporting the team's individual

Expert painter Janine Taylor hangs from a Brooklyn wall mid-project.

artistic growth and creative output, the company hosts a recurring group art exhibition for its team.

While hand-painted outdoor advertising and street art enjoy greater acceptance today, Colossal embarked on its journey at a time when public perception was still shifting. The late 1960s saw the rise of unauthorized tags, throw-ups and murals—bold expressions of identity and muted and unheard voices—yet even the most compelling pieces were often illegal and condemned. The late 1980s and 1990s witnessed a turning point as artists like Jean-Michel Basquiat, a Brooklyn native, went from gritty street walls to coveted gallery wallspace. By the 2000s, a seismic reversal started to take place: businesses that once decried graffiti began commissioning artists for their public spaces.

As an early adopter of a once-maligned art form, Colossal pioneered a novel promotional platform rooted in authentic sign-painting tradition, New York's painted advertising legacy and street culture. Hand-painted advertising and public art now thrive across Brooklyn and much of the world, a journey the company helped fuel with mural campaigns for Apple, Yves Saint Laurent, Red Bull, Nike, Coca-Cola, Gucci and other global brands.

So, as you get lost in the rich tapestry of Brooklyn, be sure to look up and around. Woven into the fabric of brownstones and boulevards are stunning hand-painted artworks. With hundreds of new murals going up each year, you might even see a Colossal landmark in the making. ∎

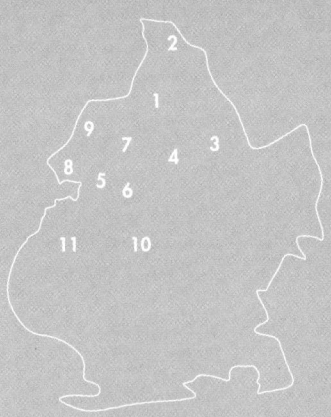

Index

Neighbor hoods

1 / Williams burg

Ponyboy
632 Manhattan
Avenue
+1 347 441 4777
→ p.8 Ⓕ

Radio Bakery
186 Underhill Avenue
+1 718 576 3800
radiobakery.nyc
→ p.87 Ⓕ

**Seven Wonders
Collective**
203 Grand Street
+1 929 337 6611
sevenwonders
collective.com
→ p.27 Ⓢ

Strange Delight
63 Lafayette Avenue
strangedelight.nyc
→ p.12 Ⓕ

Syrena Bakery
207 Norman Avenue
+1 718 349 0560
syrenabakery.com
→ p.8 Ⓕ

Taqueria Ramirez
94 Franklin Street
+1 718 576 3107
taqueriaramirezbk
.com
→ p.26 Ⓕ

Tenant
599 Manhattan
Avenue
+1 718 866 0484
tenantny.com
→ p.15 Ⓢ

The Lighthouse
58 Kent Street
thelighthouse.com
→ p.83 Ⓒ

The Lot Radio
17 Nassau Avenue
+1 347 292 7749
thelotradio.com
→ p.72 Ⓒ

Threes Brewing
113 Franklin Street
+1 731 333 3430
threesbrewing.com
→ p.64 Ⓕ

Transmitter
1329 Willoughby
Avenue, 2A
+1 646 389 9407
transmitter.nyc
→ p.34 Ⓒ

**Under the K
Bridge Park**
Gardner Avenue &
Thomas Street
nbkparks.org
/under-the-k
→ p.17 Ⓝ

Upside Pizza
640 Manhattan
Avenue
+1 718 576 3107
upsidepizza.com
→ p.73 Ⓕ

**WNYC Transmitter
Park**
Greenpoint Avenue &
West Street
nycgovparks.org
/parks/transmitter
-park
→ p.8 Ⓞ

WORD Bookstore
126 Franklin Street
+1 718 383 0096
wordbookstores.com
→ p.14 Ⓢ

Xanadu Roller Arts
262 Starr Street
+1 615 592 6238
xanadu.nyc
→ p.19 Ⓝ

3 /
Bushwick

BQ Flea
202 Meeker Avenue
+1 917 804 7258
brooklynflea.com
/bqflea
→ p.23 Ⓢ

Bunna Cafe
1084 Flushing Avenue
+1 347 295 2227
bunnaethiopia.net
→ p.79 Ⓕ

Bushwick Collective
427 Troutman Street
+1 718 366 3700
thebushwickcollective
.com
→ p.35, 37 Ⓒ

Cherry on Top
379 Suydam Street,
#3B
+1 646 927 4911
cherryontopnyc.com
→ p.7 Ⓕ

Knickerbocker Bagel
367 Knickerbocker
Avenue
+1 718 709 8888
kbbagel.com
→ p.7 Ⓕ

Lacey Burger
1329 Willoughby
Avenue
+1 718 381 4444
→ p.38, 39 Ⓕ

Lucia
2201 Avenue X
+1 718 313 0999
lucia.pizza
→ p.60, 61 Ⓕ

Ops
346 Himrod Street
+1 718 386 4009
opsbk.com
→ p.27 Ⓕ

Ornithology Jazz Club
6 Suydam Street
+1 917 231 4766
ornithologyjazzclub
.com
→ p.7 Ⓒ

Palmetto
309 Knickerbocker
Avenue
+1 718 366 2001
palmettobushwick.com
→ p.65 Ⓝ

Ra Ra Rhino
1329 Willoughby
Avenue
rararhino.com
→ p.38, 39 Ⓝ

The Broadway
1272 Broadway
+1 718 484 8353
thebroadway.nyc
→ p.13 Ⓒ

The Sultan Room
234 Starr Street
+1 718 215 0025
thesultanroom.com
→ p.75 Ⓝ

The Turk's Inn
234 Starr Street
+1 718 215 0025
turksnyc.com
→ p.75 Ⓝ

4 /
Bed-Stuy

Adanne Bookshop
115 Ralph Avenue
+1 443 507 8630
adanne.co
→ p.14 Ⓢ

Café Erzulie
894 Broadway
+1 718 450 3255
cafeerzulie.com
→ p.7 Ⓕ

Che
302 Malcolm X
Boulevard
+1 718 484 4110
che-brooklyn.square
.site
→ p.15 Ⓕ

Frog Wine Bar
358 Marcus Garvey
Boulevard
→ p.7 Ⓕ

Happy Cork
51 Buffalo Avenue
+1 347 985 9067
happy-cork.com
→ p.15 Ⓢ

Hart's
506 Franklin Avenue
+1 718 636 6228
hartsbrooklyn.com
→ p.26 Ⓕ

Liz's Book Bar
315 Smith Street
+1 718 210 2222
lizsbookbar.com
→ p.14 Ⓢ

LunÀtico
486 Halsey Street
+1 718 513 0339
barlunatico.com
→ p.7, 73 Ⓒ

Matawana
533 5th Avenue
+1 929 250 2090
matawanany.com
→ p.67 Ⓢ

Sincerely, Tommy
343 Tompkins Avenue
+1 718 484 8484
sincerelytommy.com
→ p.15 Ⓢ

The Fly
549 Classon Avenue
+1 347 405 5300
theflybrooklyn.com
→ p.56 Ⓕ

Sunny's Bar
253 Conover Street
+1 718 625 8211
sunnysredhook.com
→ p.10 Ⓝ

Red Hook Winery
175 Van Dyke Street,
Pier 41, Suite 325A
+1 347 689 2432
redhookwinery.com
→ p.10 Ⓕ

Valentino Pier
104 Ferris Street
+1 212 639 9675
nycgovparks.org
/parks/valentino-pier
→ p.10 Ⓞ

Widow Jane Distillery
218 Conover Street
+1 718 407 4927
widowjane.com
→ p.10 Ⓕ

9 /
Downtown
Brooklyn

Alamo Drafthouse
445 Albee Square
West
+1 718 513 2547
drafthouse.com/nyc
→ p.12 Ⓕ

Brooklyn Paramount
385 Flatbush Avenue
Extension
+1 718 254 9800
brooklynparamount
.com
→ p.69 Ⓒ

Center for Fiction
15 Lafayette Avenue
+1 212 755 6710
centerforfiction.org
→ p.14 Ⓒ

Gage & Tollner
372 Fulton Street
+1 347 689 3677
gageandtollner.com
→ p.39, 69 Ⓕ

Junior's Restaurant
386 Flatbush Avenue
Extension
+1 718 852 5257
juniorscheesecake.com
→ p.61 Ⓕ

Kimoto Rooftop
228 Duffield Street
+1 718 858 8940
kimotorooftop.com
→ p.7 Ⓝ

Sunken Harbor Club
372 Fulton Street, 2nd
Floor
+1 347 689 3677
sunkenharbor.club
→ p.39 Ⓕ

10 /
Flatbush

Allan's Bakery
1109 Nostrand Avenue
+1 718 774 7892
allansbakery.com
→ p.9 Ⓕ

Aunts et Uncles
1407 Nostrand Avenue
+1 347 295 0001
auntsetuncles.com
→ p.9 Ⓕ

BunNan
2123 Caton Avenue
+1 347 365 2771
bunnanbk.com
→ p.9 Ⓕ

**Flatbush Central Carib-
bean Marketplace**
2123 Caton Avenue
+1 718 282 2500
flatbushcentral.com
→ p.9 Ⓕ

Kings Theatre
1027 Flatbush Avenue
+1 718 856 5464
kingstheatre.com
→ p.9 Ⓒ

Lips Cafe
1412 Nostrand Avenue
+1 347 240 4439
lipscafebk.com
→ p.9 Ⓕ

Peppa's Jerk Chicken
791 Prospect Place
+1 718 450 3976
peppasonline.com
→ p.9 Ⓕ

11 /
Sunset Park

Bitter Monk
68 34th Street
+1 718 369 0000
bittermonk.com
→ p.65 Ⓝ

Brooklyn Grange
850 3rd Avenue
+1 347 670 3660
brooklyngrangefarm
.com
→ p.16 Ⓞ

**Kai Feng Fu Dumpling
House**
4801 8th Avenue
+1 718 437 3542
kaifengfubrooklyn
.kwickmenu.com
→ p.9 Ⓕ

Sabor de Colombia
4601 5th Avenue
+1 929 810 2395
colombianrestaurant
brooklyn.com
→ p.9 Ⓕ

Shan
191 Smith Street
+1 347 294 4660
shannyc.com
→ p.67 Ⓕ

Tacos El Bronco
4324 4th Avenue
+1 718 788 2229
tacoselbronco.com
→ p.9 Ⓕ

12 /
Other

Bar Bête
263 Smith Street
+1 347 844 9950
barbete.com
→ p.7 Ⓝ

Bay Ridge Pizza
7704 5th Avenue
+1 718 680 5405
bayridgepizza.com
→ p.56 Ⓕ

Bien Cuit
721 Franklin Avenue
+1 347 795 4328
120 Smith Street
+1 718 852 0200
biencuit.com
→ p.7 Ⓕ

Books Are Magic
225 Smith Street
+1 718 246 2665
booksaremagic.net
→ p.14 Ⓢ

Brennan and Carr
3432 Nostrand Avenue
+1 718 769 1254
brennanandcarr.com
→ p.59 Ⓕ

**Brooklyn Botanic
Garden**
990 Washington
Avenue
+1 718 623 7200
bbg.org
→ p.17, 38 Ⓞ

Brooklyn Flea
80 Pearl Street
+1 718 928 6603
brooklynflea.com
→ p.23 Ⓢ

Brooklyn Grange
Brooklyn Navy Yard,
Bldg 3, Clinton and
Flushing Avenue
+1 347 670 3660
brooklyngrangefarm
.com
→ p.16 Ⓞ

Brooklyn Museum
200 Eastern Parkway
+1 718 638 5000
brooklynmuseum.org
→ p.68, 69, 78 Ⓒ

Burrow
68 Jay Street, Suite
119
+1 718 875 4820
burrow.nyc
→ p.7 Ⓢ

Cafe con Libros
724 Prospect Place
+1 347 460 2834
cafeconlibrosbk.com
→ p.14 Ⓕ

Café Mado
818 Franklin Avenue
+1 718 484 4110
cafemado.com
→ p.26 Ⓕ

Caputo Bakery
329 Court Street,
Carroll Gardens
1 718 875 6871
caputobakery.com
→ p.54 Ⓕ

Central Library
10 Grand Army Plaza
bklynlibrary.org
+1 718 230 2100
→ p.4 Ⓒ

Court Street Bagels
181 Court Street
+1 718 624 3972
→ p.7 Ⓕ

Daybreaker
daybreaker.com
→ p.74 Ⓒ

Only the Dead Know Brooklyn

Thomas Wolfe

Dere's no guy livin' dat knows Brooklyn t'roo an' t'roo, because it'd take a guy a lifetime just to find his way aroun' duh goddam town.

So like I say, I'm waitin' for my train t' come when I sees dis big guy standin' deh—dis is duh foist I eveh see of him. Well, he's lookin' wild, y'know, an' I can see dat he's had plenty, but still he's holdin' it; he talks good an' is walkin' straight enough. So den, dis big guy steps up to a little guy dat's standin' deh, an' says, "How d'yuh get t' Eighteent' Avenoo an' Sixty-sevent' Street?" he says.

"Jesus! Yuh got me, chief," duh little guy says to him. "I ain't been heah long myself. Where is duh place?" he says. "Out in duh Flatbush section somewhere?"

"Nah," duh big guy says. "It's out in Bensenhoist. But I was neveh deh befoeh. How d'yuh get deh?"

"Jesus," duh little guy says, scratchin' his head, y'know—yuh could see duh little guy didn't know his way about—"yuh got me, chief. I neveh hoid of it. Do any of youse guys know where it is?" he says to me.

"Sure," I says. "It's out in Bensenhoist. Yuh take duh Fourt' Avenoo express, get off at Fifty-nint' Street, change to a Sea Beach local deh, get off at Eighteent' Avenoo an' Sixty-toid, an' den walk down foeh blocks. Dat's all yuh got to do," I says.

"G'wan!" some wise guy dat I neveh seen befoeh pipes up. "Whatcha talkin' about?" he says—oh, he was wise, y'know. "Duh guy is crazy! I tell yuh what yuh do," he says to duh big guy. "Yuh change to duh West End line at Toity-sixt'," he tells him. "Get off at Noo Utrecht an' Sixteent' Avenoo," he says. "Walk two blocks oveh, foeh blocks up," he says, "an' you'll be right deh." Oh, a *wise* guy, y'know.

"Oh, yeah?" I says. "Who told *you* so much?" He got me sore because he was so wise about it. "How long you been livin' heah?" I says.

"All my life," he says. "I was bawn in Williamsboig," he says. "An' I can tell you t'ings about dis town you neveh hoid of," he says.

"Yeah?" I says.

"Yeah," he says.

"Well, den, you can tell me t'ings about dis town dat nobody else has eveh hoid of, either. Maybe you make it all up yoehself at night," I says, "befoeh you go to sleep—like cuttin' out papeh dolls, or somp'n."

"Oh, yeah?" he says. "You're pretty wise, ain't yuh?"

"Oh, I don't know," I says. "Duh boids ain't usin' my head for Lincoln's statue yet," I says. "But I'm wise enough to know a phony when I see one."

"Yeah?" he says. "A wise guy, huh? Well, you're so wise dat someone's goin' t'bust yuh one right on duh snoot some day," he says. "Dat's how wise *you* are."

Well, my train was comin', or I'da smacked him den and dere, but when I seen duh train was comin', all I said was, "All right, mugg! I'm sorry I can't stay to take keh of you, but I'll be seein' yuh sometime, I hope, out in duh cemetery." So den I says to duh big guy, who'd been standin' deh all duh time, "You come wit me," I says. So when we gets onto duh train I says to him, "Where yuh goin' out in Bensenhoist?" I says. "What numbeh are yuh lookin' for?" I says. *You* know—I t'ought if he told me duh address I might be able to help him out.

"Oh," he says, "I'm not lookin' for no one. I don't know no one out deh."

"Then whatcha goin' out deh for?" I says.

"Oh," duh guy says, "I'm just goin' out to see duh place," he says. "I like duh sound of duh name"—Bensenhoist, y'know—"so I t'ought I'd go out an' have a look at it."

"Whatcha tryin' t'hand me?" I says. "Whatcha tryin' t'do—kid me?" *You* know, I t'ought duh guy was bein' wise wit me.

"No," he says, "I'm tellin' yuh duh troot. I like to go out an' take a look at places wit nice names like dat. I like to go out an' look at all kinds of places," he says.

"How'd yuh know deh was such a place," I says, "if you neveh been deh befoeh?"

"Oh," he says, "I got a map."

"A *map*?" I says.

"Sure," he says, "I got a map dat tells me about all dese places. I take it wit me every time I come out heah," he says.

And Jesus! Wit dat, he pulls it out of his pocket, an' so help me, but he's *got* it—he's tellin' duh troot—a big map of duh whole goddam place wit all duh different pahts. Mahked out, you know—Canarsie an' East Noo Yawk an' Flatbush, Bensenhoist, Sout' Brooklyn, duh Heights, Bay Ridge, Greenpernt—duh whole goddam layout, he's got it right deh on duh map.

"You been to any of dose places?" I says.

"Sure," he says, "I been to most of 'em. I was down in Red Hook just last night," he says.

"Jesus! Red Hook!" I says. "What-cha do down deh?"

"Oh," he says, "nuttin' much. I just walked aroun'. I went into a coupla places an' had a drink," he says, "but most of the time I just walked aroun'."

"Just walked aroun'?" I says.

"Sure," he says, "just lookin' at things, y'know."

"Where'd yuh go?" I asts him.

"Oh," he says, "I don't know duh name of duh place, but I could find it on my map," he says.

"One time I was walkin' across some big fields where deh ain't no houses," he says, "but I could see ships oveh deh all lighted up. Dey was loadin'. So I walks across duh fields," he says, "to where duh ships are."

"Sure," I says, "I know where you was. You was down to duh Erie Basin."

"Yeah," he says, "I guess dat was it. Dey had some of dose big elevators an' cranes an' dey was loadin' ships, an' I could see some ships in drydock all lighted up, so I walks across duh fields to where dey are," he says.

"Den what did yuh do?" I says.

"Oh," he says, "nuttin' much. I came on back across duh fields after a while an' went into a coupla places an' had a drink." "Didn't nuttin' happen while yuh was in dere?" I says.

"No," he says. "Nuttin' much. A coupla guys was drunk in one of duh places an'

started a fight, but dey bounced 'em out," he says, "an' den one of duh guys stahted to come back again, but duh bartender gets his baseball bat out from under duh counteh, so duh guy goes on."

"Jesus!" I said. "Red Hook!"

"Sure," he says. "Dat's where it was, all right."

"Well, you keep outa deh," I says. "You stay away from deh."

"Why?" he says. "What's wrong wit it?"

"Oh," I says, "it's a good place to stay away from, dat's all. It's a good place to keep out of."

"Why?" he says. "Why is it?" Jesus! Whatcha gonna do wit a guy as dumb as dat? I saw it wasn't no use to try to tell him nuttin', he wouldn't know what I was talkin' about, so I just says to him, "Oh, nuttin'. Yuh might get lost down deh, dat's all."

"Lost?" he says. "No, I wouldn't get lost. I got a map," he says.

A map! Red Hook! Jesus!

So den duh guy begins to ast me all kinds of nutty questions: how big was Brooklyn an' could I find my way aroun' in it, an' how long would it take a guy to know duh place.

"Listen!" I says. "You get dat idea outa yoeh head right now," I says. "You ain't neveh gonna get to know Brooklyn," I says. "Not in a hunderd yeahs. I been livin' heah all my life," I says, "an' I don't even know all deh is to know about it, so how do you expect to know duh town," I says, "when you don't even live heah?"

"Yes," he says, "but I got a map to help me find my way about."

"Map or no map," I says, "yuh ain't gonna get to know Brooklyn wit no map," I says.

"Can you swim?" he says, just like dat. Jesus! By dat time, y'know, I begun to see dat duh guy was some kind of nut. He'd had plenty to drink, of course, but he had dat crazy look in his eye I didn't like. "Can you swim?" he says.

"Sure," I says. "Can't you?"

"No," he says. "Not more'n a stroke or two. I neveh loined good."

"Well, it's easy," I says. "All yuh need is a little confidence. Duh way I loined, me older bruddeh pitched me off duh dock one day when I was eight yeahs old, cloes an' all. 'You'll swim,' he says. 'You'll swim all right—or drown.' An', believe me, I *swam*! When yuh know yuh got to, you'll do it. Duh only t'ing yuh need is confidence. An' once you've loined," I says, "you've got nuttin' else to worry about. You'll neveh forgit it. It's somp'n dat stays with yuh as long as yuh live."

"Can yuh swim good?" he says.

"Like a fish," I tells him. "I'm a regular fish in duh wateh," I says. "I loined to swim right off duh docks wit all duh odeh kids," I says.

"What would yuh do if yuh saw a man drownin'?" duh guy says.

"Do? Why, I'd jump in an' pull him out," I says. "Dat's what I'd do."

"Did yuh eveh see a man drown?" he says.

"Sure," I says. "I see two guys—bot' times at Coney Island. Dey got out too far, an' neider one could swim. Dey drowned befoeh anyone could get to 'em."

"What becomes of people after dey have drowned out heah?" he says.

"Drowned out where?" I says.

"Out heah in Brooklyn."

"I don't know whatcha mean," I says. "Neveh hoid of no one drownin' heah in Brooklyn, unless you mean a swimmin' pool. Yuh can't drown in Brooklyn," I says. "Yuh gotta drown somewhere else—in duh ocean, where dere's wateh."

"Drownin'," duh guy says, lookin' at his map. "Drownin'."

Jesus! I could see by den he was some kind of nut, he had dat crazy expression in his eyes when he looked at you, an' I didn't know what he might do. So we was comin' to a station, an' it wasn't my stop, but I got off anyway, an' waited for duh next train.

"Well, so long, chief," I says. "Take it easy, now."

"Drownin'," duh guy says, lookin' at his map. "Drownin'."

Jesus! I've t'ought about dat guy a t'ousand times since den an' wondered what eveh happened to 'm goin' out to look at Bensenhoist because he liked duh name! Walkin' aroun' t'roo Red Hook by himself at night an' lookin' at his map! How many people did I see get drowned out heah in Brooklyn! How long would it take a guy wit a good map to know all deh was to know about Brooklyn!

Jesus! What a nut *he* was! I wondeh what eveh happened to 'm, anyway! I wondeh if someone knocked him on duh head, or if he's still wanderin' aroun' in duh subway in duh middle of duh night wit his little map! Duh poor guy! Say, I've got to laugh, at dat, when I t'ink about him! Maybe he's found out by now dat he'll neveh live long enough to know duh whole of Brooklyn. It'd take a guy a lifetime to know Brooklyn t'roo an' t'roo. An' even den, yuh wouldn't know it all. ∎

Thomas Wolfe was a celebrated American author known for his lyrical, autobiographical prose. Born in 1900 in Asheville, North Carolina, he gained fame with Look Homeward, Angel *and explored themes of identity and place. His short story* Only the Dead Know Brooklyn, *written in 1935, captures the borough's mystery and immensity.*

Available from LOST iN

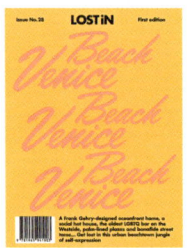   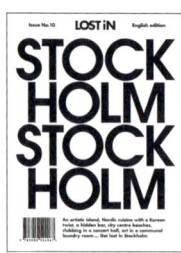 

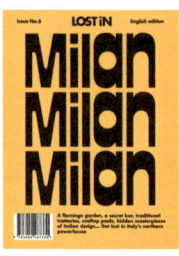    

Shop the City Guides at www.lostin.com

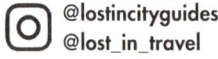 @lostincityguides
@lost_in_travel

LOSTIN.COM